"Understanding individual differences in perception is crucial to coaching, and it is our core mission at Birkman International. I know Nathan and Dianne's experience and heart will help coaches and their clients experience real success."

—Sharon Birkman, President and CEO, Birkman International

"*Real Coaching Success* couldn't be any clearer or more informative. It is well written and very practically applicable. Honored to recommend!"

—Tom Ziglar, CEO, Ziglar, Inc., and proud son of Zig Ziglar

"Caring for yourself before you can take great care of your clients is counter-cultural. *Real Coaching Success* will help the new coach getting started, the veteran coach wanting to re-invent themselves, and everyone in between.

Nathan and Dianne's revolutionary approach to coaching will help any new or experienced coach better understand how to care for themselves so that they can best serve the clients that they care for. Slowing down enough to examine yourself will help a coach unlock the best version of themselves."

—Kevin Harris, President, Radical Mentoring

"Authentic, clarifying and inspiring! Whether you are a coach or exploring becoming one, you'll gain clarity around what coaching is and isn't, the motivations and energy it requires, and what drives the best coaches to excellence.

With humility, the Baxters use their own growth stories to offer the reader their hard-earned wisdom—it's pure GOLD! I experienced these truths first hand when I engaged Dr. Baxter as a coach and it led to my own journey into professional coaching. Here's some free coaching advice: Read this book!"

—Sharon Mankin, Leadership Coach, Lead Self Lead Others, LLC

"Real Coaching Success is a must-read for anyone wanting to build a coaching business and do it with excellence. The Baxter's show their personal heart for people and share their professional experience. They allow us to benefit and lead ourselves and our clients well."

—Dr. Rodney Agan, Founder/Connexus Group

"Nathan and Dianne are not only veteran leadership coaches, experienced with a broad array of industries, but Nathan is one of the very best trainers I've ever encountered. If you are looking for one book to accelerate your coaching practice, look no further. This is it!"

—Dr. Rod MacIlvaine

"For many years I've seen Dianne and Dr. Baxter's love of helping others reach their potential. Through Nathan's vision and Dianne's enthusiastic friendship, I learned to respond to mentoring requests with courage and confidence. Dianne and Nathan have been, and continue to be, a life-changing force. If you're serious about moving your story forward as a coach, this book is your next chapter."

—Keil Cadieux, grateful friend and mentor

"Real Coaching Success is a breakthrough resource for both new and seasoned coaches. It's practical, proven, humorous, and personal. I have had the privilege of watching Nathan and Dianne live out what they have written in this book, and the huge success they've had. As a coach myself, I view this book as the new gold standard for coaches who want to excel in their craft."

—Dave Jewitt, Founder, Your One Degree

"Authentically connecting with others to help them reach their potential is a high calling. Dianne and Nathan's book defines real coaching success and brings much-needed professionalism (and heart) to those interested in results."

—Kari Mirabal, International keynote and TEDx speaker, Author, and Networking Consultant

"When I first started working with Nathan and Dianne, I had experienced great success in my field, yet I was totally burned out and frustrated. Dr Baxter's coaching techniques not only supported me in getting back on track, they also gave me the clarity and focus to lead myself better, take my next step forward with confidence, and do what we all want to do—get better and GROW! The Baxters have an incredible ability through speaking truth and asking practical questions, to support those they are coaching, as they work through the emotional hang ups and fogginess that most leaders go through at some season in their lives. I highly encourage you to plug into their amazing process."

—Jan Thetford, National Sales Director, Mary Kay

"Nathan and Diane define coaching and what success looks like. With plenty of personal and practical examples, they chart the course. The Baxters have charted what great coaching is! The book includes plenty of questions, encouragement, growth exercises, truth-telling, and accountability."

—David Fletcher, Founder, XPastor

"Nathan and Dianne know what it means to help someone move their story forward. Dr. Baxter guided me through a trying time as I transitioned from an executive to board director at QuikTrip."

—Christopher Cadieux, investor, speaker, and board director at QuikTrip Corp.

"Coaches, listen up! I have been involved internationally in high-performance sport for over 15 years. Show me a coach who doesn't want coaching success! Rarely have I met a coach who leads themselves with the same amount of effort that they give to their athletes. I recommend this book to any leader who pours their life into their people and can often find themselves with an empty tank and lack of focus. After working with Nathan and Dianne I feel energized to dream big again. Their book will give you clarity on how to live *on purpose, for purpose* leading you into real coaching success!"

—Sarah Bradley Young, Director of College Women's Ministry, Global Golf

"Nathan and Dianne have had a profound influence on my leadership and coaching journey. *Real Coaching Success* removes the mystery of coaching for novices and compels longtime coaching practitioners to practice simplicity, intentionality, and excellence in further developing their coaching practice. This is a must-read, top-shelf coaching resource that will inspire and elevate every coach!"

—Amie Gamboian, CEO/Executive Coach, Who You Are© Leadership Coaching & Consulting

Real Coaching Success

What it Takes to Be an Excellent Coach and Build Your Business

Dr. Nathan Baxter and Dianne Baxter

Real Coaching Success

What it Takes to Be an Excellent Coach and Build Your Business

Dr. Nathan Baxter and Dianne Baxter

© Copyright 2020, Lead Self Lead Others, LLC. All Rights Reserved.

Cover design and layout: www.MikeLoomis.CO

No part of this book may be reproduced, stored in a retrieval system, or transmitted by any means without the written permission of the author and publisher.

Published by Lead Self Lead Others, LLC ®

Case studies in this book have been modified and combined with other stories for illustrative purposes. Names and details have been changed. Our companies never disclose any information about our coaches or clients without express written permission.

RealCoachingSuccess.com

Dedication

To all those who mentored, coached, and befriended us on our journey.

To our growing family of coaches, who inspire us every day.

To our clients who give us the honor of serving them.

Thank you!

Contents

Introduction	1
Chapter 1: Real Coaching Success is Simple	15
Chapter 2: The Most Important Ingredient	27
Chapter 3: Care and Feeding of a Successful Coach	37
Chapter 4: Your Unique Power	45
Chapter 5: Who to Coach or Not to Coach?	53
Chapter 6: Professionalism: What are Your Motives and Standards?	61
Chapter 7: Professionalism: Do You Have Clear Coaching Objectives?	71
Chapter 8: Professionalism: Coaching Skills for Real Success	79
Chapter 9: Professionalism: Calibrate and Re-Calibrate for Real Success	91
Chapter 10: Do I Have Enough Coaching Tools?	101
Chapter 11: Your Coaching Success	107
Authors	115
Glossary of our coaching terminology	119
Appendix A	125
Appendix B	128
Appendix C	130

Introduction
The Story Behind the Stories

You might have something to say, but does anyone want to listen?

"So, I'm curious, Dave. Why are we meeting?"

This was our third 6 a.m. meeting at a local diner. As a twenty-eight-year-old husband, new father, and youth pastor, I wasn't used to getting up this early. But something about our breakfast meetings captivated me, and it sure wasn't the pancakes.

"I just thought you could use a friend, Nathan," he answered with his disarming smile.

This was a new concept for me: somebody wanted to invest in me—without a complaint or agenda. (At the time, my job involved fielding frequent complaints and a steady stream of helpful suggestions from parents of those I mentored.) His generosity made a big impression. He asked questions and seemed to actually care about my answers.

"Where do you see your life in five years?"

"What are some areas holding you back in life, that you'd like to work on?"

Dave was fourteen years older than me, but he was miles ahead of me in terms of his career and moving his life story forward.

I don't know what's happening at these meetings, I thought. *But wow—this interaction is bringing me alive. It's challenging me to see my life differently.*

I didn't realize it at the time, but I was being coached.

For weeks, I never missed a Thursday breakfast meeting and I was never late—no matter the weather. Setting the alarm for a 5 a.m. wake up was difficult—Dianne and I had our first baby at the time—but we agreed that I'd be absent from the morning routine once a week. She saw how beneficial the time with Dave was for me, and I believed she saw how the investment made a difference in my life as a husband and father. Someone was investing in me—on purpose—and I could sense I was growing.

Little did I know at the time, but Dave was figuring out this "mentoring thing" as he went along. Because I engaged with his questions, followed up on his recommendations, and was hungry to learn, he started searching for more ways to help me. One year into our coaching, he asked his brother-in-law, Paul Stanley for advice and he recommended the book, *The Making of a Leader*, by Bobby Clinton. Dave immediately bought a copy and handed it to me at our next breakfast meeting.

I devoured the book, and was especially captivated by an exercise detailed in chapter two called a "timeline." The following week I said, "I really want to do the timeline, but I want you to do yours, too. Okay?" He smiled, but also looked a bit embarrassed. Dave hadn't read the book and he had no idea what I was talking about.

After a good laugh, and a quick review of the exercise, we decided to invite a few other guys to a two-day retreat and share our individual timelines with one another.

And they said yes.

The Keystone Group

A few weeks later, in January 1993, seven of us met at a relative's condo at nearby Lake Keystone. I was as excited as I was nervous. After all, no one—including Dave and me—had actually *completed* the timeline exercise, nor shared it with another person. Each attendee had an hour to present his timeline to the group. Despite the fact that Dave and I knew next to nothing about leading a gathering like this, the experience was successful beyond our imagination.

Whether we like to admit it or not, sharing our story is extremely important to every human being. To tell your story—even a self-edited version—to others who are interested, is always constructive. To share something painful about your life, in a safe environment, brings perspective and healing. In particular, men don't "share" very well, and don't often have the opportunity.

Everyone who attended the gathering agreed to meet again the following January for another timeline review, and focus on the progress each person had made. (By the way, the Keystone group still meets every year.) Not only was this exercise personally helpful for me, but the experience of using a simple tool to help others was a lightbulb moment. And that's when I began to think about being more intentional in developing people. It's one thing to finish a project well, or finish a week well, but what about finishing our *lives* well?

If it was possible to help people in a significant, lasting way—utilizing proven tools and techniques—I believed it was also possible to develop *excellence* in doing so. But I still wasn't sure how to do this, or what to call it.

What Do We Call This?

The following year Dave's brother-in-law, Paul, co-wrote a book with Bobby Clinton called *Connecting*.[1] The authors had researched mentoring relationships by studying both the mentee and the mentor, and developed a continuum which located eight different categories of mentoring.

Mentoring styles ranged from active to passive, but closer to the active side of the spectrum—and in the "intensive" category—was the word "coach." Prior to seeing the distinctions in styles, I tried to be like Dave and follow his approach. As you might predict, this led to mixed results. After all, we're different people. My style was more "intensive" and I learned that Dave was more relational in his interactions—which is Dianne's style. When I read the definition of coach/coaching in the book, it immediately hit home. *This is me!*

Here's how Paul Stanley and Bobby Clinton defined "coach:"

"The Coach's central thrust is to provide motivation and impart skills and application to meet a task or challenge."

From that point on, I called myself a coach. I finally had the right word for what I wanted to do—and it perfectly fit my personality.

A few years later, I developed my own definition:

> Coaching is the intentional effort to come alongside another person to help them experience their full potential. It is a forward-thinking activity that uses a combination of questions, encouragement, growth exercises, truth-telling, and accountability.

---

[1] https://www.amazon.com/Connecting-Mentoring-Relationships-Spiritual-Formation/dp/0891096388/

A sense of connection to the title of "coach" is crucially important—for you, and for your clients. You must appreciate your motivation to help people before anyone else will. And you need a term that communicates this in a clear way. For Dianne and me, it's other-oriented, intentional, with the goal of making progress toward potential. You need a definition you're comfortable with, whether it's teacher, mentor, manager, disciple-er, advisor, or coach.

To be effective, and experience real coaching success, you must be very confident and comfortable in your initial interactions with potential clients. For us, the title is coach. Over the past 30 years, the use of the word has evolved from a precise description—usually describing those involved in helping athletes—to a more broad meaning.

This is another reason why you must not only wear the title with confidence, you must be able to define what that title means to those you coach.

Nathan the Coach

Interestingly, as a youth pastor—and later a senior pastor—once I was equipped with the self-bestowed title of coach, I suddenly felt free to bring the weight of "coaching" to my staff, and some of my key volunteers. Since my staff really had no choice in the matter, recruiting them as "clients" was pretty straightforward—even for me.

"Hey, I want you to come see me once every other week so I can *coach* you and help you do your job better."

With every person I coached, I learned more about what worked—and what didn't work.

People put up with me and my newfound title for a couple months. I hadn't developed *custom* coaching yet, so my one-size-fits-all approach simply didn't fit. And I even managed to offend some people in the process.

One of my staff was so *uninterested* in the opportunity to be coached by me that we agreed to limit our one-on-one meetings to once a month . . . for a maximum of five minutes . . . and not even sit down!

Dianne had a similar reaction to my "coaching." And I finally learned a key lesson: not everyone wants to be coached . . . by me.

But as time went on, I also added more and more tools to my toolbox, found proven ways to customize my approach for each client, and constantly improved them based on every coaching experience.

Seven Years Later

Meanwhile, as you might have guessed, I wasn't the only person Dave was mentoring. For the next seven years Dave and I continued to meet every other week, as the impact of our (elementary) coaching spread. This was unplanned, unorganized, and far from strategic—but our coaching was authentic and impactful. Surprisingly one dynamic of our work began to stand out. Complete strangers called me and asked, "I heard about how you're working with my friend. Could you work with me?"

I only had one phrase (finishing well) and one primary tool (the timeline) but everyone with whom I shared these concepts experienced similar growth.

One morning a close friend, Drew Files, and I were comparing notes about our timelines, when we said to each other, "This is so much fun. Let's tell everybody we know!"

We invited about one hundred men to New Life Ranch (a local retreat center) for a one day event. And one hundred people made the two-hour drive to attend. The response was so overwhelming we recruited the Keystone group to help facilitate, because we needed people who were familiar with the timeline tool.

Our agenda consisted of one piece of paper that explained our concept of finishing well, and one piece of paper with a sketch of a timeline. We called the gathering "Live a Meaningful Life." (Yeah, we were pretty impressive in those days.)

But once again, we struck gold. As those in attendance engaged with the concepts, the timeline, and each other, the energy was palpable. The event proved to us how hungry people were to be intentional with their lives—and how willing they were to share with others.

They simply needed a path—and a guide.

It never occurred to me to charge people for my time—just as it never occurred to Dave to have me pay for any of our breakfasts—

or his time—over the course of our first several years. We were having too much fun investing in others.

By the way, most people would think it's easy to "sell" free coaching. But those people have never tried it.

Dianne the Coach

Before my (Nathan's) church career progressed, and before our two boys were born, Dianne decided to make a career transition.

In college, she started a business with an international cosmetics company while earning a marketing degree from Oklahoma State University. After graduation, she landed a job in the marketing department of a large company, was very successful, and soon earned more money than me. But after a few years, we both wanted to start a family. Returning to self-employment was an appealing option for her.

With her business acumen and relational style, her enterprise grew quickly. She loved the work, enjoyed setting and reaching goals, and we needed the second income. Her drive came from a God-given desire to help people experience personal growth and success while building their own business. She was—and is—a gifted communicator with a sincere interest in developing people. And her listening skills made her an excellent salesperson and coach.

I'll state the obvious: Dianne was successfully coaching people—as a key element of her career—for years before I even knew how to spell the word coach. She coached in person, on the phone, and at sales meetings across the country.

A year later our son, William was born, and our son, Connor was born nineteen months later.

Fast forward to today: our two sons—and their wives—have been actively meeting one-on-one with young people and investing in their lives since college. They grew up around coaching and developed their own style of coming alongside others to see them develop in their potential. They married girls who shared the same passion to help others. It's been a great blessing to be a family that shares the joy of helping others on their journey. We fully anticipate our grandkids will catch the coaching bug. The tools and techniques we've developed help coaches and clients of *all* ages!

Paying the Price

As my career took me to Kansas City, and eventually back to Tulsa, I continued to coach staff, volunteers, and whoever my schedule allowed. Looking back, it was almost like my career became a way to fund my volunteer coaching passion. Being a coach actually *cost* me time and money. But I loved it.

Every week, I spoke with good people who had amazing potential. But they were not focused. These were people I respected and liked, but they were just going through the motions. When I asked them, "What's your idea of finishing well?" they didn't have an answer. So I reverse-engineered the discussion by explaining what *finishing* well means and how you need to be *living* well.

"What does living well mean to you?" I'd ask.

Once they began to answer—or attempted to answer—I found tremendous opportunity to offer my coaching perspective and became more confident in my pitch. "One of the things I do, in addition to my full-time job, is meet with people like you and help them focus their lives. I have a process I take clients through. And by the way, you didn't answer my question very well. I can help you with that, too!"

Most responded the same way I responded to Dave. When someone is intentional about helping you experience a great life, you'll usually receive an enthusiastic, yes. Even though I wasn't strategic about building a business—or even trying to build one. Coaching was a passion and I was becoming good at it.

Honestly, I never even thought about charging for my time. For Dianne and me, our payment came in different currencies. When you happen to see a coaching client at a restaurant and their spouse thanks you for the difference you've made in their lives—that's a pretty good paycheck.

As Dianne's career blossomed, we would occasionally meet together with her peers in the company. These women were already successful leaders, but they were curious about how I coached corporate leaders and became interested in emerging best practices from other industries, which I'd been studying and applying. As I shared some insights in one gathering at our home over a Christmas brunch, one of Dianne's colleagues got tears in her eyes. She knew she needed to lead her team better, and wanted to grow. We decided to meet once a week, where I would offer some teaching on leadership to the group

After each meeting at a coffee shop around the corner from our house, I'd send an email follow-up with a synopsis of the lesson and practical action items. Unknown to Dianne and me, these leaders forwarded those emails to their network. After a few weeks, more and more top leaders in the cosmetics company asked to be put on my email list. Within a few months, my list grew to over 1,600 people and required several hours a week to administer. The "Pinkspirations" newsletter was born, eventually going out to several thousand women per month.

The takeaway? People are hungry to learn how to experience a better life and more successful careers. As a new coach, or someone who is considering becoming a coach, it's easy to doubt this hunger exists. But if you don't believe, the growth of your coaching business will suffer.

After a few more years in my role as executive pastor, my sideline coaching schedule started to fill up. I'd squeeze in calls with someone on the East coast in the morning, and those on West coast in the late afternoon after work for in person meetings, we utilized Friday afternoons and Saturdays, simply because those were my two days off.

Dianne and I knew we provided value, but we never connected coaching to a dollar amount. Besides, I was pretty committed to my profession, and my salary paid the bills. These weren't long-term coaching engagements. We'd meet four or five times and move the client on their way. Because of her successful career over the past 30 years—and starting over in a new city—Dianne knew that coaching excellence was connected to business growth.

As the years went by, I had built an array of tools, diagrams, articles, and other resources for coaching clients. For example, a client might ask, "How do I process grief?"

"I don't know, but I'll get back with you," I'd answer. And I did get back to them—with the most helpful information I could find, and an offer to help them walk through the process.

In my filing cabinet, the work files were beginning to shrink and my coaching files were growing—fast. It was a visual representation of the place coaching had taken in my life. The funny thing is, I wasn't really aware that there was a coaching "industry," didn't know any of the terminology, or what others were doing in the space. We were simply trying to help people.

And the referrals kept coming. One day, as I was scheduling an appointment for a new client, I noticed my first available meeting time was five months out. I'll confess that my schedule—and coaching practice—might have continued this way indefinitely, if it wasn't for a stubborn client named, Jim.

Jim and the Big Breakthrough

"Nathan, I want to pay you for coaching me, and helping me make all this progress," Jim said as I walked him to his car after a coaching session at my home.

"Well, I don't take money," I replied.

"I'm going to pay you anyway!" Thankfully, he was more stubborn than I was—and probably smarter. He handed me an envelope, shook my hand, and got into his car. Once I was back inside I closed the front door and opened the envelope. As I pulled out the check, I couldn't believe my eyes. Jim had paid me five hundred dollars, which felt like ten thousand dollars at the time.

I walked—no, *floated*—into the dining room where Dianne was doing paperwork. "You're not gonna believe this," I whispered as I handed her the check.

"What's this for?" she asked, with a puzzled-but-pleased expression.

"For coaching this guy! Can you believe it?"

"But we don't charge for coaching people."

"Evidently we do now."

We'd been coaching people for many years, and our thinking changed radically that day. Our coaching practice was about to change as well.

Are You a Life Coach?

I'll admit it. We kept that check in a prominent place on the dining room table for a few days before cashing it. Our heads were spinning as we considered the prospect of me actually earning a living by doing something I loved to do.

Dianne and I started having conversations about our life and business that we'd never had before. We started to dream about possibilities.

Could we actually work together? Have more fun? And help people in significant ways?

Could our God-given desire to help people reach their potential align with our love of hospitality?

Should we tell our friends about this? How about our extended family?

That's when I started looking around to see what other people were doing in the coaching industry. And that's when I came across the term, "life coaching."

I'm definitely not doing that, I thought.

The concept struck me as very passive. Many practitioners seemed to be unsuccessful in their careers, but now, with the added title of "life coach" they were suddenly a bastion of wisdom—for a fee. Many didn't have expertise, tools, or a track record of results. By this time, I'd earned a doctorate degree and had a deep appreciation for rigorous research and application. I was disappointed with the lack of professionalism in the "life coaching" arena.

They had business cards and web sites.

All I had were tools and referrals from those we'd helped.

As part of our due diligence, I met with an "official" life coach and explained my vision for building my business: two-day sessions with follow-up appointments—in coffee shops, at my home office, or by phone. After hearing my ideas, he paused, grinned condescendingly, and said, "Let me be honest with you, Nathan, based on my years of experience. That's never going to work."

"Well," I said, with an even bigger grin, "I've been doing exactly that for the past two years." Although we both called ourselves coaches, my approach and vision was from a different universe. I saw value in what he was offering, but I knew we could never adopt his concept of coaching.

Even though Dianne and I enjoyed coaching, and saw success, we knew we needed more techniques, more professionalism, and a framework to help more people with customized solutions.

Counting the Cost

Based on our research, overflowing calendar, the $500 check, and positive feedback we'd received, Dianne and I had a business meeting. We decided that if we could build my coaching business to 70 percent of my salary, I'd leave my day job and become a full-time coach. That might sound like a fun meeting, and it was. But it also involved a hard look at our monthly expenses—including the reality of eliminating all non-essential spending.

We were willing to sacrifice 30 percent of our lifestyle to take a journey of faith. And our company, Lead Self Lead Others, was born in 2009.

That decision was much easier to stomach than the next, more pressing one. I needed to change my pitch from "No charge!" to "What's in your wallet?" My coaching revenue had to go from zero to something—and fast.

Nonprofit means no profit. I'd been in that arena for 28 years, and had perfected the art of making *no* money from coaching. The transition to paid coaching was very awkward for me.

My pitch didn't change, and my process didn't change, but the price had to change. Conversations with potential clients continued as usual, until the question, "What do you charge?"

In my next coffee meeting with a potential client, he looked me in the eye, told me he needed what I offered, and asked about the fee.

"Five hundred dollars per hour," I confidently declared.

Just kidding. I completely choked. For the next four meetings with potential clients, I reverted to the "no cost" answer. At this rate, I'd never get to 1 percent of my salary, let alone 70 percent!

Two more months into my new moonlighting "career" and my total sales were zero. By the third month, I had closed a few engagements for a few hundred dollars.

My next big meeting was with a business executive who heard about my work and wondered if I could help him and his team. As he answered my questions, I thought, *I can help this guy—and I have the necessary tools.* Then he asked the fateful question.

"What's it going to cost us?"

Thankfully, muscle memory didn't overtake my mouth. Numbers raced around my brain. *$500? $2,500?* Finally I said, "Let me get back with you tomorrow, okay?"

That afternoon I tried to craft an email reply with the right number. After an hour of agonizing between doubt, belief, free and a fortune, I finally called the executive.

"Rob, I gotta be honest with you. I'm new on the corporate side of the industry and really don't know what to charge. Would you mind helping me understand your budget?"

Now it was his turn to say he'd get back with me. As I ended the call, my heart sank. *Did I just torpedo this opportunity? He must see right through me and realize I have no idea what I'm doing.*

A few minutes later my email beeped with a message from Rob.

"Nathan. Our budget for what we discussed is only $15,000. Does that work for you?"

Trying to hide my excitement, I replied to Rob with a polite "Yes, I believe we can work with that amount."

Then I yelled to Dianne. "Book a dinner reservation—we're going out tonight!"

Coaching Myself

When I saw what the market was paying for coaching, another shift in our thinking occurred. *If Rob's gonna spend this amount of money, he might as well spend it with me!* That revelation turbocharged my confidence, and my interactions with potential clients.

Make no mistake about those $500 and $15,000 paydays; I was lacking in the billing department, but had been delivering excellent coaching for many years. Those experiences simply motivated us to align our rates with the level of professionalism and results we delivered.

Four months after Dianne and I agreed on the 70 percent trigger, I handed a resignation letter to my employer. Stuff just got real, as they say. On one hand, I had 40 more hours a week to fill up with paying clients. On the other hand, I had 40 more hours a week to fill up!

We don't describe this transition as a leap of faith; it was a decision to follow our calling. But there was risk involved. *What happens if the referrals stop?* I didn't have a marketing strategy to lean into.

Our business plan was to deliver excellence and help people. It still is.

When you consider the nature of coaching, you realize it isn't about having never-ending client relationships. The moment you start, a sunset is coming. My backup plan was a job at Home Depot. Maybe I'd be able to buy tools at an employee discount.

For us, in that moment, it was riskier to *not* follow our calling than to stay where life was "safe." *I was a coach.* If I worked at Home Depot, I'd still be Nathan the coach. I'd helped over two hundred people; they saw results and that meant something to us. Nothing else compared with the exhilaration we felt seeing people's lives and careers improve.

It was go time.

Coaching Coaches

Five years later, I started having to turn away business because of all the referrals. I could have taken on a few more clients, but the quality of my service would have suffered. The goal of a business is to make a profit, but there's only so much of you and your time. I had to start thinking like a business owner instead of some guy with a business card and a calendar. That's when we decided to share what we'd learned with other coaches and with those interested in becoming a coach. After all, Dave's investment in me transformed my thinking and my career, and ultimately led to the development of my coaching practice that included excellent tools, which have helped thousands of people.

So we contacted four people who we knew were interested in building a coaching practice based on our values and model for excellence. "We're not charging anything, so you'll probably get what you pay for. And we've never certified anyone, but let's try this!" Each person agreed to give our prototype coaching certification program a try.

We met the chosen four coaches twice a month for six months and tried to pour everything we knew into them. The process was unorganized, spontaneous, and an absolute blast!

In the years that followed, word spread that we offered training for coaches unlike anything on the market. Once again, our phones and email started buzzing. We couldn't refer people to other training in good conscience; if there were any programs we were proud to recommend we would have done so. In our opinion, they were too expensive, contained content primarily focused on theory, and were not practical enough. That's when we decided to expand our focus and commit to helping those who wanted to coach. I love researching theory and have the degrees to prove it, but we wanted to equally focus on the nuts and bolts of building a business that pays the rent.

Real Coaching Success was born.

This book is the result of that decision, and thousands of lessons learned—the hard way—in our coaching journey.

Dianne and I had our fair share of challenges and mistakes, but our businesses, our coaching, and this book, are the product of our partnership, experience, and shared wisdom.

We wrote this introduction from my (Nathan's) perspective because—as you've seen—my learning curve was steeper. In the chapters that follow, our voices are combined for easier reading, and because that's how our coaching businesses operate.

As we step into the practical aspects of building a successful coaching business, know there is hope. You—and your clients—can experience real coaching success. But it will take commitment and work. We often give our coaching team at Lead Self Lead Others the following motivational speech: "Be awesome or don't coach." This is the same standard Dianne and I hold ourselves to during our daily company debrief. The last thing we want to do is report how we did a *good* job coaching that day; we want to share stories of delivering *excellence*.

We're not just making candles here. Coaching can change peoples lives for the better.

Are you ready for Real Coaching Success?

Chapter 1
Real Coaching Success is Simple

We are students of the person sitting in front of us.

We don't hold any assumptions about you or your coaching journey, but we do have a few crucial presuppositions about professional coaching. You can acquire the skills to become excellent. You can be successful regardless of your style. There is far more demand for coaching than there are excellent coaches.

Coaching is not counseling. Although coaching and counseling have similarities, counseling focuses on repairing what has been damaged before moving forward. Coaching focuses on the *future* and helping a client move toward their full potential. But a person's story does play a very important role in the coaching process. We want to help a person live well and finish well. But the way we relate to a client can have a profound impact on their progress.

Real coaching success is simple, but it's not easy.

Varying Views and Voices

If you've researched coaching for ten minutes, you already know there are many views about what works and why. We've certainly learned a lot from other coaches through the decades, but we've also developed very strong opinions and practices from our experience. With respect to other voices on the subject, we owe it to you to point out a major distinction regarding the coaching relationship dynamic.

In a nutshell, we don't approach a coaching relationship as a "journey together" as co-equals. Rather, we—and our network of certified coaches—believe we need to provide something our clients do not have, and we are there to deliver. We lean more toward the importance of having a level of expertise or experience that we can share with our clients. We are not trying to develop a friendship, although we are friendly.

In my work coaching executives, many have expressed a concern that previous coaches they have worked with had no leadership experience, and certainly not executive level experience. Needless to say, the coaching engagement didn't last long. If you are going to position yourself as a guide for someone else you have to know where you are going and possess the résumé to back it up.

We're certainly not saying a coach must have executive experience. But they must have some leadership experience—and success—especially in the area of self-leadership.

In the book, *Co-Active Coaching*, the authors describe the coaching relationship in which "the coach and coaches are active collaborators." They continue, "In Co-Active coaching, this is a relationship—in fact an alliance—between two equals for the purpose of meeting the coachee's needs." Although we agree with them, we feel that some coaches take their definition too far.[2]

We feel it's important to help the coaches we're training to be really clear on what is "two equals" and what is not. We agree we're two equals in terms of being on a journey in life; both can share stories and learn from each other. But we also feel strongly that the coach should be offering something the client cannot do for themselves. We have found that "the answer lies within" approach isn't always true. They simply need someone to tell them. Sometimes a client genuinely doesn't know what they don't know.

However, we wholeheartedly agree with their stand on truth-telling. "It can be handled with sharpness or softness, but it confronts the usual tacit acceptance of the clients explanations... A real relationship is not built on being nice; it's built on being real."

Every successful coaching relationship is built on mutual respect. In our companies, we believe a coach needs to bring specific experience and expertise that the client does not possess. When I buy a new car, I don't *collaborate* with the car dealer, I purchase a car in order

---

[2] *Co-Active Coaching. Changing Business Transforming Lives,* 3rd edition. House, House, Sandahl, Whitworth.
https://www.amazon.com/Co-Active-Coaching-3rd-Changing-Transforming/dp/B00DWBN12I/ref=sr_1_2?dchild=1&keywords=coactive+coaching&qid=1586961291&sr=8-2

to obtain something I value. I need the car dealer to tell me what I don't know about the car.

Coaching Is:

Growth assignments versus suggestions.

Agreed upon accountability.

Pushing and pulling forward versus merely being on a journey together. (As noted above, we believe the coach needs to be the expert in the room when it comes to life change.)

A defined set of coaching objectives versus "safe" conversations.

It's about *progress* versus presence.

I like the following distinction stated on the Harley Therapy Counseling Blog: "A coach is focused on your potential, versus a counselor is focused on helping you be at peace with yourself and your life. Coaches are trained in helping clients move forward in life, versus counselors who are trained in human development, sexuality, family dynamics, and mental health conditions."[3]

At our companies, Lead Self Lead Others and Real Coaching Success, we have a stronger expression of truth-telling and holding clients accountable to move forward. There are various schools of thought in coaching as to whether or not you should let the client discover the answer. We teach a different approach. If we see something they need to discover about themselves or next steps they need to take, we simply tell them!

One of our company values is: "We are truth tellers. We value client discovery but we do not shy away from telling them the truth. We believe truth is what people are really seeking."[4] Wouldn't you agree?

(To read our company values, go to www.LeadSelfLeadOthers.com)

Coaching is the intentional effort to come alongside another person to help them experience their full potential. It is a forward-thinking activity that uses a combination of questions,

---

[3] Dr Sheri Jacobson, "What's the difference between counseling and coaching?" February 23, 2017, accessed January 5, 2020, https://www.harleytherapy.co.uk/counselling/coaching-and-counselling.htm

[4] www.leadselfleadothers.com

encouragement, growth exercises, truth-telling, and accountability for their self-leadership.

Coaching is about helping a person continue to move their story forward. Life is a journey through various seasons that affect us in different ways. It is normal to get stuck, disoriented, and distracted from our true purpose and potential.

A great coach is one with a huge amount of *professional curiosity*.[5] We are curious and interested in a person's story, their current reality, their potential, and whether or not they have a vision for their life.

Real coaching success does not come from merely taking people through a program. Rather, we are willing to do the hard work to develop a unique coaching plan based on what we keep learning about the client. The first step in creating a coaching plan is to establish the coaching gap. This being the gap between their current reality and their potential.

We are students of the person sitting in front of us. What are the questions I should be helping our clients answer? Here are just a few of our favorite questions that help us coach with excellence.

- What is your story?
- What are your passions, fears, and aspirations?
- Have you embraced your unique identity?
- How well are you living up to your potential?
- What does *living* well look like to you?
- What is holding you back from the life you really want to live?

Working to answer these types of questions begins to inform us as to the client's reality and their true potential.

Ken Blanchard makes the case that managers who adopt a coaching style need to be focused on what's inside the person you are coaching. "Servant leaders feel their role is to help people achieve their goals. They constantly try to find out what their people need to

---

[5] The term "professional curiosity" was coined by Dr. Rod MacIlvane who is a certified coach with Lead Self Lead Others, LLC.

perform well and live according to the vision. They bring an emphasis on bringing out the magnificence in people."[6]

The most effective managers do genuinely care about each of their people. But they imbue care with a distinct meaning. In their minds, to care means to set the person up for success. Every great manager I've ever interviewed has this approach. No matter what the situation, their first response is always to think about the individual concerned and how things can be arranged to help that individual experience success.[7]

Coaching is paying attention and responding accordingly.

Misconceptions About Professional Coaching

Misconceptions hinder progress. For potential clients, this might mean they have the wrong idea about what coaching is. You can help change that. For coaches, wrong thinking about professional coaching will unnecessarily limit you—and your bank account.

Many aspiring coaches don't believe they can make a full-time career in the profession. That's simply not true. But the hard fact is, to earn an excellent income you'll need to continually increase your excellence as a coach.

Another misconception is the idea that money will fuel your passion or skill. After all, the enormous energy it takes to coach has to be fueled somewhere. But money cannot be your fuel. Your motivation and passion must be found in developing people and seeing them reach more and more of their potential.

So we ask you this important question: "If you were not able to earn a living coaching, would you still coach people?" (We would!)

Marketing will build your coaching business, right?

Wrong. Think of your favorite restaurant. Chances are you didn't visit for the first time based on an ad, but based on a referral or review. A "good" meal won't inspire people to tell their friends. But when you have an amazing dining experience, you want to tell your

---

[6] Ken Blanchard, *Leading at a Higher Level*. (Upper Saddle River, New Jersey: Blanchard Management Corporation, 2015), 262. For an excellent resource on bringing coaching into the corporate setting check out *Helping People Win at Work* by Gary Ridge Ken Blanchard.

[7] *First, Break all the Rules* / Gallup. p.231

friends. It's the same with coaching: be amazing or be out of business. If business isn't good after a year or two as a coach, don't blame your marketing. You might want to examine your level of skill and professionalism—and invest in some training.

Many struggling or aspiring coaches sabotage their own success because they believe people don't want or need what they offer. Again, this simply isn't the case. The reason heart surgeons will always have a job is because everybody has a heart. It's the same way in coaching. Every person needs to be in touch with their purpose, but so many are not. When a gifted and skilled coach starts exploring a client's heart, they always find potential and purpose. Too often, the client is out of touch with their own potential and purpose. What a privilege to help them connect and move forward!

Finally, many coaches assume more paying clients will translate into a successful career. You can get a dollar from anybody—once. Earning the *second* dollar is what separates an amateur from a professional.

But how does a professional coach handle the money side of the business?

What Are Your Rates?

Another breakthrough on our coaching journey occurred when we finally figured out our rates. We say rates—plural—because we learned you need a variety of rates because you'll work with a variety of people at different income levels and who have different needs. Every entrepreneur needs to land on their numbers. This doesn't mean anyone will pay the rate you establish, but it's important to start somewhere.

One of the areas we always need to help coaches with is how to figure out their rates. And "rate" is code for "I have to deal with my insecurity," because if I'm going to charge you a certain amount, it means I'm placing my value at that amount. If you value what you deliver on the low end of the rate-scale, you will struggle to charge the right amount. We help coaches understand if they will provide their coaching service in the manner in which we train them, the value is worth more than what you might ask.

Once we got over the fear of establishing our fees, we tried a coaching package investment of $500 which included a certain number of sessions. Once we had our rate and package fee established, a small number of potential clients—maybe 5 percent—said, "I want to work with you. We honestly don't have the money." You can decide to gift some coaching at that point and receive what I (Dianne) call a "paycheck of the heart," but you must not change your standards for coaching. Why is this so crucial? Because referrals—whether the referrer paid you or not—are the lifeblood of your enterprise.

If we won the lottery tomorrow, we'd still coach people. Money is not the driver. So pre-decide how much coaching you can give away, and stay with it.

Last week, I (Nathan) invited a guy from an exercise class to breakfast. I'd been working out alongside him for three years, sensed a coaching opportunity, and had a genuine desire to gift my time. I handed him my card and said, "I'd like to buy you breakfast some time." A few days later, we sat down at a restaurant and the first thing he told me was, "I can't believe you invited me. I went to your website, and, um, I don't have any purpose. Would you help me?"

We met again the following week and he insisted on paying me something for my time. "There is no way you're paying me," I told him. "This was a friend invite. I just happened to be a coach. We'll call it divine coincidence."

Receiving his money would've ruined the whole gig for me.

Imagine this progression in your coaching business:

- Who can I coach for free? I want to build my skills.
- Coaching can't be free. This is my business.
- Business is so good. Who should I coach for free?

If this sounds interesting to you, it's because this is our story. And it can be your story.

Why Getting Paid Is a Win-win

New or aspiring coaches often have the wrong mindset about money—particularly when it comes to being paid for their expertise.

Let's consider the reality of charging for services, and why payment is a true win-win.

I don't know about you, but when I take a moment to consider the fact the someone has pulled money out of their bank account and sent it to me, my level of attention, preparedness, and sharpness increases dramatically. There are many other places they could have chose to invest their money, and I want them to see a huge return on their investment. Every engagement is an opportunity to live our integrity. How we prepare, coach, and follow up—when the client isn't looking—will make or break your coaching practice.

On the other side of the table, a paying client *should* bring the same focus and discipline to the engagement. We've coached hundreds of people—for free and not for free. In general, when someone pays, they show up with their homework completed. If not, they have the opportunity to learn a valuable lesson at no extra charge when I smile and say, "You just paid me a lot of money to say 'See you next week'!"

We—along with our team of coaches and students—believe we provide the absolute best coaching, which produces the greatest results. Because we actually believe—and live out—our excellence, we don't blink when it comes to charging a premium. There is an audience for coaches with a high level of preparedness, research, experience, and integrity. And we train and certify coaches for this audience. (We also train coaches who want to intentionally give their services away, because the same standards of excellence apply.)

In our experience, payment increases truth-telling—from all parties. We don't coach to make friends or have nice conversations. We coach because we're called to help people move toward their potential.

When you earn a living from coaching, you can help more people. When you're paid well, you can create margin to provide remarkable services—and go the extra mile.

About a year ago, Thomas, a former client, in Colorado, contacted me (Nathan) about a career transition. I happened to be in there on business, so we met at a local coffee shop.

"What do you think about me becoming a coach?" he asked with a nervous smile.

"I think you'd be awesome!"

"What does it really take?"

After listing a few important skills and practices, I told him, "Believe it or not, you've been coaching for a long time. And you're a natural. You just need some structure and a toolbox. But if you want to transition into a full-time coaching practice, I'll be the first in line to help you."

Fast forward six months, and this newly-certified coach went public with his new career. A week later he left me a voice mail. "Nathan and Dianne. Just calling to tell you I landed my first client, and I'm holding a big check in my hands." To help someone transition through a career change, and to hear the excitement in their voice, is thrilling.

As were were writing this chapter, Julie—one of our certified coaches—sent us a photo of herself with a college student she was coaching. They had just finished her timeline, and the student said the experience changed her outlook on life. Julie's coaching business is going so well, she can invest in young people who don't have the resources to pay for coaching. There's no telling how many people she will help.

Moving Your Story Forward

Your clients will face resistance, failures, successes, and a growth curve. And thankfully, you're there to help them move their story forward. In your coaching business, you're also writing a story. You'll have setbacks and successes as you seek professionalism and excellence. We're here to help you.

Coaching is an unregulated industry, and—unfortunately—there is no standard of excellence. If we were human resources professionals, medical professionals, attorneys, physicians, or CPAs we'd be required to attend continuing education classes to retain our credentials. Frankly we believe some coaches should have their license revoked . . . if only they had a license! That's why we're working to set standards of excellence that deliver results for customers. In the chapters to follow, our goal is to make a significant contribution to you—and the coaching industry as a whole. Excellence needs to be defined.

Additionally, and because there are too few credible resources, new and aspiring coaches need to understand proven business models and best practices for professionalism. Together, Dianne and I have over 40 years of coaching experience, and receive questions every week about real coaching success. The answers to those questions are in your hands, and in our courses.

If you were to attend one of our workshops, and asked us if you were on a successful track as a coach, we'd offer the following statement:

Real coaching success is simple: Are you receiving referrals?

We said it's simple, but it's not *easy*.

Questions for the Coach:

What are your biggest fears about coaching others toward their full potential?

_____

_____

_____

_____

_____

_____

_____

What are five words that represent the coaching standards or values you have for yourself?

_____

_____

_____

_____

_____

_____

_____

_____

Bonus: Email us your coaching standards to: office@realcoachingsuccess.com and we will give you some feedback.

Chapter 2
The Most Important Ingredient

If you don't lead yourself well, you can't lead others well.

Have you heard the joke about the coach who was always late, but was relentless in holding his clients accountable for their time management? Me neither. Because it's not funny.

Do you want real coaching success? Then you need to lead yourself well.

If you don't lead yourself well, you can't lead others well. So if you don't coach yourself well, you will always struggle to coach others well. Coaching is such an other-oriented exercise, it's best to have yourself taken care of and out of the way. If you're not managing yourself very well, you will be a distraction. We recommend all our coaches maintain a relationship with a mentor or coach who continually pushes toward their full potential.

If you asked us if we could help you become a successful coach, our answer is "yes." And we would start by having you answer a few questions: "Are you leading yourself well? And how do you know you're leading yourself well?"

What Is Self-Leadership?

We define self-leadership as, "stewardship." In other words, what are you doing with what you have been given? Do you know what to do, when to do it, and are you willing to do it? Coaches who lead themselves well consistently answer yes and demonstrate a pattern in their work week that affirms their answer. Their lives model intentionality—living on purpose, for purpose.

Coaching and mentoring others is a very other-oriented practice. The only way you can really be good at coaching is to always be observing, listening, and actively processing what you are experiencing as you engage with your client. If you do not take care of yourself emotionally, physically, and spiritually you will be distracted in the engagement—your career and your client will both suffer.

"Mentoring is a dynamic process, not a static, one-size-fits-all program. It involves a journey that is active, vibrant, and ever-changing because people are complex, changing, unique individuals, not static commodities that fit neatly into a box with expected outcomes geared to strict timetables."[8]

The goal of self-leadership as it relates to coaching is to lead yourself out of the way so you can focus on the client.

Do you know what you need to be at your best? This is where all coaching success really begins.

In a survey we conducted with over two thousand respondents, they indicated the five most important areas of their lives that required high levels of self-leadership: habit, health, relationships, time, and money. Knowing this has informed our coaching practice, and helped us move people forward in all areas.

Know self; lead self. Know others; lead others.

Coaches with high levels of self-leadership are defined by the following: they know what to do, when to do it, and are willing to get it done. They put themselves in a position to coach others well. They have become committed to living up to their full potential which can only be accomplished by living an intentional life.

If you're not awesome, you won't receive referrals. To be an awesome coach, you have to have the right motives. And—if you're human—this doesn't always come naturally. So in order to help you find success, let's start with your motives for coaching.

The Motivation of Self-Leadership

Have you ever stayed at a nice hotel or restaurant and asked a staff member for something?

"Absolutely!" is often the answer. And, "At your service." Or even worse, "My pleasure." But too often, the response is not genuine; it's the result of corporate service-industry training. The words are

---

[8] David A. Stoddard with Robert J. Tamasy. *The Heart of Mentoring. Ten proven principles for developing people to their fullest potential.* (Colorado Spring, CO: Navpress, 2003), 48

there, but the motivation or sincerity is often lacking—so the overall experience suffers. To provide exceptional value and service there has to be a very sincere motive: *I'm here to serve you. And I really mean it.*

What's really driving you to meet with people, offer them truth, and work on their behalf? What motivates you to prepare and follow up with extra mile excellence?

We all have deep, sometimes hidden, motivation for our endeavors. Have you taken an honest look at your motivations—and are you comfortable with what you see? It's okay if you find a mix of "good" and "bad" reasons for coaching. Here are some examples of common motivations that—once you face them—will help you move toward higher personal integrity.

- Do you need to be needed?
- Do you want to be portrayed as an expert?
- Do you like to be liked?
- Do you love hearing yourself talk?
- Is it the money?

Your motives inform your behavior. Your motives affect your emotions. How do you act and feel when the pressure is on? If money is your driver, you will likely avoid telling some hard truths to a client for fear of ending the paid engagement. Take a hard look at your behaviors and emotions regarding coaching and you can address motivations that need to go.

Why are pure and well-considered motivations so key? When you experience challenges on your coaching journey, you'll want to revisit your core reasons for being a coach. When you have an unpleasant interaction with a client, you can ask yourself, "Why am I doing this?" And happily—you'll have a great answer that will help you serve with excellence and joy.

I'm in the business of helping people, and there's a person in front of me now. My assignment is clear. I'm going to help them.

We never judge the motivations of those we train to become a certified coach, but we can predict whether or not they will build a successful career. We have to be in touch with our motives because coaching is not always easy.

Coaches with the right motives coach for one reason: to help the client move toward their potential. Right motives empower you to create impact beyond your wildest dreams. To place your mind, heart, and emotions into a position to serve, you must lead yourself well.

It's tough to help a client with their finances when you're in constant short-term debt because you don't manage your money well. You can't give what you don't have.

Fear of Coaching

Tom came to see me (Nathan) based on a friend's referral. He convinced me over a cup of coffee that he was passionate about coaching. He shared a couple terrific stories of transformation, and seemed to enjoy meeting with people.

We took him through a six-month certification process. He graduated and we launched his marketing campaign. After four months he had not landed one single client. We revisited his plan to promote himself and it was solid. After another month, and no paying clients, so we dug a bit deeper.

Tom understood coaching, believed he could provide tremendous value, and was well-rehearsed in presenting himself as a coach. But when it was time to take center stage and pitch a prospective client, fear took over and he didn't share the next step to engagement. For some people, this is a big problem. But why?

Let's be honest, approaching—or responding to—someone about your coaching practice is an exercise in vulnerability. New coaches, or those who don't believe their résumé is impressive enough, doubt themselves. Sadly, this doubt keeps them from connecting with people they could help—and keeps them from gaining valuable experience along the way.

Many aspiring coaches who find themselves challenged by insecurity choose to pursue some letters at the end of their name. They believe some "certification" will give them the confidence boost they crave, and somehow make their services more appealing to potential clients.

It won't.

The vast majority of people who enter the coaching arena, and want to take their business to the next level, simply need to lead themselves well to overcome excuses and face their fears. Yes, Real Coaching Success offers certification, resources, and workshops. This training and mentoring builds skills and professionalism on the foundation of your passion to help people.

If you have a deep desire to help people using the vehicle of coaching, you must view the journey—and learning curve—as a matter of *stewardship*.

When your passion to help people is the driver, you'll keep moving forward—past fear and self-doubt.

Some letters behind your name will not make the difference—for you or your clients.

When I'm tired, feeling insecure, or the thought of losing a client creeps in, I don't fall back on the letters behind my name. I remind myself, *I'm called to do this. What an amazing business to be in, the business of life-transformation!*

Leading Yourself Means Preparation

Real coaching success reminds me of watching an Olympic track and field event. The athletes don't just walk up to the line and wait for the starting gun. They perform dozens—maybe hundreds—of mental and physical movements to prepare. (In addition to the years of disciplined training that brought them this far.) Once in position, they take time to place their feet and fingers in the precise location they need to begin the race well. This is a picture of what a good coach does—or should do—prior to every coaching engagement.

When the client enters—boom!—it's on. An impactful coaching session starts *days* before we even meet with a client. That's self-leadership in action.

Case Study: What Would You Do?

There are times when our personal lives can be a bit chaotic or stressed. Human beings have limits.

A few months ago I (Nathan) faced a perfect storm that caused serious coaching fatigue: a major home remodel, a growing backlog of client follow-up, and unexpected events in our personal schedules. I could feel it. I was out of gas.

I reviewed my schedule and noticed I had coaching calls set for the next morning. What would you do in this situation? (I'll tell you later.)

Perfect Coaches

We're not looking for perfection, and neither are clients. I don't need to coach people who are perfect. I need them to be in an intentional process of moving their story forward.

If you're not leading yourself well, there's a high probability you're tired, rushed, unprepared, and emotionally needy. Those are distractions that take you away from the high focus required for your client.

Here's a simple example. Have you ever caught yourself checking your phone while in a client meeting? You're kidding yourself if you don't think the client notices. But that's not even the point! Self-leadership means we bring our best. We focus on the client 100 percent, whether we're at a coffee shop or on the phone. There's a difference between listening and *active* listening, and active listening requires discipline—and practice. Excellent coaching requires concentration and critical thinking. Therefore, self-leadership is very important.

When the start of the race sounds, you're ready to focus and bring what the client needs.

Sometimes It *Is* about You

Coaching isn't about you, but sometimes it *is* about you. We can model self-leadership—and the struggle—by sharing personal experiences, successes, and failures. When you're all-in on the journey of leading yourself well, you'll have valuable insights to share with others.

If I'm working on goal setting with one of my clients, I might say, "Let me tell you one of my goals for this year . . . " This exchange lets the client know I'm on the journey with them. Or I might share an area where I'm pushing myself, which will explain why I don't feel sorry for them—or buy their excuse—at the moment. You can't offer any stories or helpful lessons if you're faking it and not living it.

One of the biggest mistakes in coaching is presenting yourself from the perspective of who you *want* to be instead of who you really are. Others can sense your lack of confidence and comfort.

We have a hunch that you as a human being have a certain ability. It's a God-given ability to discern whether or not someone is authentic. We all can sense, at some level, when a person is trying to hide something, or being insincere, or has insecurities. The point is, your client can sense, at some level—if you're not leading yourself well. Clients have to be extremely comfortable with who you are, and this starts with you being comfortable with how you're leading yourself.

You have to know who you are. One of the best ways to figure out who you are is to be really clear on who you're *not*. Chisel away everything you're not and—*voilà*—there you are!

If a client asks to meet me (Nathan) before 9 a.m., I already know the answer. *Not happening.* Why? I don't do well before nine, so the coaching appointment won't go well. Simple. And this practice for me leads to a genuine win-win engagement. (I do sometimes make exceptions, for example, when a client is a surgeon and has little schedule flexibility.)

Who am I to put such constraints around my schedule? I'm someone who wants to deliver awesome service.

I don't know

When a client asks you a question to which you don't have an answer, are you comfortable admitting that you don't know? Or do you have a habit of filling the air with the sound of your wisdom, and hope an answer eventually emerges?

(*No, you can't answer these question with, "I don't know."*)

This can be a difficult situation for a new coach, especially if you've worked hard to prepare for the session, and feel the pressure of delivering for a paying client. The smartest answer is, "I don't know. But let me think about it and get back with you."

This is another reason why motivation is so important. If your motivation is to impress, you'll try to make up an answer. You'll know you are making up the answer, and—on some level—so will the client. Seasoned leaders deal with this every day, and they can smell a cover-up a mile away. To lead yourself well, be honest with yourself. If you don't know, you don't know. Then be honest with your client. People respect honesty.

Lead Yourself by Being Yourself

Coach from your natural personality. Know your style and be yourself in any formal coaching engagement so the client can experience you, and your method of coaching.

When you know—and intentionally operate in—your unique personality, you'll connect with your natural giftedness, which will help you be more effective as a coach.

Coaching is challenging enough on its own. Why make it harder by trying to coach in a style you picked up from someone else?

This has been our criticism of many coaching certification programs. They use a one-size-fits-all training and do a poor job of helping the coach truly understand who they are—which has a direct bearing on their style of coaching as well as who their target clients should be.

The key is to focus on the coaching objectives and then use your instincts and skills to move toward the objectives.

Lead yourself well by being yourself.

Case Study: Here's What I Did

Earlier in this chapter I shared a story about being overwhelmed and exhausted—and realizing the next morning I had a scheduled coaching appointment. What would you have done?

Here's what I did. I texted the client: "Hey, I need to move our call a day or two. Lots going on and I'm not at my best this week."

That was a difficult text to send, but I was more nervous about not delivering excellence than receiving a potentially negative reaction from the client. Excellent coaching requires concentration and critical thinking. Therefore, self-leadership is very important. Before you try to lead your client, be sure to lead yourself well.

Reflect on your most recent coaching appointments. Were you prepared? If not, can you trace the core reason back to a lack of self-leadership? You need self-leadership to ensure you take care of your own needs: Every good coach leads themselves well by focusing on:

- Time margin: so you can feed your spirit, soul, and body
- Money margin: so you can have pure motivation and the ability to be generous
- Emotional margin: so you can focus on your client and help them move forward.

"The core problem with working longer hours is that time is a finite resource. Energy is a different story. Defined in physics as the capacity to work, energy comes from four main wellsprings in human beings: the body, emotions, mind, and spirit. In each, energy can be systematically expanded and regularly renewed by establishing specific rituals—behaviors that are intentionally practiced and precisely scheduled, with the goal of making them unconscious and automatic as quickly as possible."[9]

One of the most amazing results of coaching through the lens of self-leadership is how much your own life will improve along the way!

---

[9] Manage Your Energy, Not Your Time. Harvard Business Review. FROM THE OCTOBER 2007 ISSUE. Tony Schwartz & Catherine McCarthy

Questions for the Coach:

Do you lead yourself well? Explain your answer.

What changes do you need to do a better job of leading yourself well?

Chapter 3
Care and Feeding of a Successful Coach

If you don't care for yourself well, you can't care about others well.

Coaching is draining.

Yes, coaching is rewarding, exhilarating, and sometimes fun. But the very nature of coaching, as we see it, involves giving out. Whether realized or not, all coaches give of themselves in three main areas: emotionally, physically, and spiritually.

When you engage with a client, it's like hooking them up to your batteries. The more you prepare, talk, and follow up, the more drained you'll be. Try this for several hours a day, and you'll be toast by Thursday. This puts you in a very dangerous position of not being awesome—unless you recharge.

Recharging Your Emotions

Coaching is the art and discipline of being intentional about the person in front of you. Focusing on—and caring about—another human being is mentally taxing. How do you replenish yourself emotionally?

No, we're not going to give you a list of things to do. (Self-leadership means discovering what recharges you.) Besides, you don't need another to-do list. But you do need to know—and *do*—what it takes.

How well do you know yourself? For example, can you name the top three activities that energize you? Can you also list three specific activities that drain you? And, specifically, what do you *need* in your day to operate at your full potential?

All our coaches are required use the Birkman® Assessment tool—personally—so they can begin to understand their unique wiring with extreme clarity. Only then can they lead themselves well. (If interested in how you and your coaching business can benefit from the Birkman® Assessment tool, please contact us.)

You've been given a unique set of abilities and needs. But if you don't know them, how can you be a good steward of your one and only life? Here are a few examples of just how we use the tool to help with self-leadership.

Nathan: I've found that because I score a very high "outdoor interest" score that it is helpful to spend time outdoors before, during, and after coaching sessions. (I built an outdoor office where I can meet with clients). Because my most productive style of work is task orientation, versus people or relationship orientation, I work best when I coach a client using a checklist of conversations I plan to have with them.

Dianne: I on the other hand have a natural orientation toward people and relationships. I like to work on the coaching relationships for the first ten minutes of a coaching session. As the connection is established, I shift to coaching conversation related to coaching objectives. As an example of self-leadership, I have a high need for time alone. Therefore, I've learned that I can only coach so many people in any given day.

Recharging Your Body

To actively listen, your body has be involved. If your body runs out of energy, you'll know it, and your client will know it. Coaching is a sport.

If you think about it, the only way to be really good at coaching is to be really good at being fully engaged in each moment of a coaching session. Some of the professional athletes I have coached have taught me that for them to play at the top of their game they place more emphasis on the work *before* the game than the work they do *during* the game. Preparation is key to their success—mental preparation, physical preparation, and emotion preparation.

We often forget that the human body is a limited resource. It depletes, and needs to be re-energized. So if you're not eating healthy, not sleeping, and not using your time well there is a direct bearing on your confidence, energy, and your ability to coach. If you're not taking care of yourself physically, a client will notice. This might even make a client doubt your ability to guide them.

If you stay up till two in the morning and have a breakfast appointment the next morning, will you be able to bring 100 percent to the table? Of course not. But the real question is, *Are you comfortable bringing only 80 percent?* And, *Why would you not do everything in your power to bring 200 percent?*

Real coaching success is not about perfection. You don't need to be an Olympic athlete to coach. But you must apply intentional, consistent stewardship to your life and business.

How do you replenish yourself physically? Again, you must find the answer for yourself. But we will remind you that the human body is amazing and requires both exercise and rest to operate at its best.

Recharging Your Heart

If you're a coach, and a person of faith, there are some resources made available to you that others don't have. If you're a person of faith, the question is, *Are you utilizing and practicing what you believe?*

Faith, in a nutshell, means you believe someone is out there who knows you—and is someone you can have a real relationship with. Everyone has faith. Some people don't know how to articulate it clearly. If you believe there is *no one* out there, that's a solid faith position as well.

We're not here to judge anyone's faith, but we are very interested in knowing about what a person believes. We always ask our coaching clients, and coaches we have the privilege of training, *What is your faith background?*

We're Christians, and we used to ask if someone was a Christian. It was an innocent and well-intentioned question, but ignorantly phrased. We never intended to make any client or coach uncomfortable, we simply wanted to know more about a vital part of who they are. We also want to show respect to people who believe differently than we do. "What is your faith background?" can be a wonderful question to ask in order to understand more about your client.

For coaches we train, we ask, "What is your faith background, and how do you plan to incorporate your faith in your coaching?"

If faith is important to you, why wouldn't you want to intentionally integrate it into your coaching? Our job is to help you reach your full potential. If your faith is a part of who you are, then we need to help you incorporate it.

So, once again, the question becomes, *How do you replenish yourself spiritually?* And, *Are you practicing what you believe?*

Time: The Natural Resource for Self-Leadership

Self-leadership takes time, and involves some control over time. It takes time to coach, and it takes time to care for yourself—emotionally, physically, and spiritually.

We're motivated to be very efficient in our use of time because we believe in the power of preparation. Have you ever considered how many minutes you invest in a one-hour coaching session? Add up all the hours:

- Talking or emailing with someone referring you
- Preparing for a "simple" introduction
- Creating the proposal (and reviewing it before sending)
- Answering questions from the client
- Setting up the first appointment
- Preparing for each appointment
- The appointment
- Organizing notes
- Emailing the resources in a follow-up note to the client
- Scheduling the next appointment
- (And between every step above: *thinking* about the client!)

A quick estimate of the list above will show that a sixty-minute engagement means hundreds of minutes of your time and energy. A mediocre coach puts their brain in the game a few minutes before the appointment—either they're not managing time, or they haven't truly counted the cost of excellence.

Margin, in all areas of life, is not a luxury. Margin is a necessity.

Money Margin

You don't need to be a billionaire to be a coach. You can have a mortgage and a car loan—and maybe even an "easy monthly payment" on that boat. But to be a successful coach you must manage your money as well as you can. And as with any area of life, it's a process.

In training coaches, there are four areas we assess when it comes to finances.

- Are you earning what you're worth? (Or selling yourself short?)
- Are you giving some of the money you earn away? (Or is coaching all about *getting*?)
- Are you putting some money into savings? (Stuff happens. Are you ready?)
- Are you spending the rest of your money in a way that makes sense, and living within your means?

Money, and lack thereof, can be a major source of stress. Coaches who aren't paying attention to their finances, will not reach their full potential. Debt is a weight. Place fifty-pound backpacks on Olympic sprinters and their time will slow—even if they makes it to the finish line.

This isn't a time management or money management book. But this is a book about real coaching success, which requires that we lead ourselves well. Not perfectly, but with consistent effort. Anything you can do to be a better steward of your time and money will make you a better coach. When you're a better coach, you'll help transform the lives of more people. And you'll transform your own life.

The highest form of leadership is leading by example. But let's be clear; we're not after perfection, we want to live a life that pursues potential.

What Are You Doing?

There is a story that Jesus told in chapter 25 of the book of Matthew which describes someone who gave different amounts of money to three employees—stewards—with the expectation that they would invest it and produce an increase while he was away.

The employer didn't micromanage the stewards or give them specific instructions. But when he returned, he asked each employee to give an account of what they did—or did not do—with what they were given.

One of the three was ashamed to admit that he buried the money, because he was afraid of losing any. This employee was angrily rebuked and had his position taken away. The other two produced a healthy return and were rewarded. Even though the amount of money given was different, the focus was on the relative growth they achieved. They took a risk in order to receive a return—and a reward.

Every human being has unique skills and talents. And so does every coach. You want to help your clients be the best stewards of their lives, but you must be a good steward yourself in order to build a successful business.

Questions for the Coach:

Make a list of your dreams and ideas related to coaching others, and ask yourself if you are being a good steward of those dreams and ideas.

Are you investing in your dreams and ideas, or are you playing it safe?

Chapter 4
Your Unique Power

Utilizing your unique coaching style is exhilarating. Discovering it can be a little challenging.

We, along with all the coaches we have trained, have guided almost 10,000 people through a timeline exercise. Yes, really.

The initial version of the exercise was our first—and only—coaching tool, and we used it ten years before we launched our company. We coached people through the timeline exercises in many settings: in our office, boardrooms, retreats, workshops, boats, and coffee shops. After the first few hundred, we noticed a surprising pattern.

We, and our coaches, don't push for information, we simply let the client share what comes to mind about certain periods of their life. What surprised us was how clients—across all demographics—rarely shared the positive moments, but consistently told us about the painful moments.

We consistently refined the process to make sure we weren't somehow leading them to share about hurtful, discouraging, or upsetting milestones. And still the results were the same. We had to make sense of this. After months and years of pondering and research, we landed on this conclusion:

> *Your most powerful life messages come from what you learned from your pain.*

When addressing a certain moment or season in a client's life, we'll often ask, "You learned something profound from this—that no one can take away from you—didn't you?" For fellow faith-based clients, we help them answer the question, "What did God teach you through that experience, spirit to spirit?"

But we also make the crucial distinction that experience is *not* the best teacher. Rather, evaluated experience brings knowledge, wisdom, and personal growth. In coaching we not only identify life-shaping events, but we then probe to see if clients have evaluated the experience, by asking them:

- What did you learn about yourself through the experience?
- What did you learn about others?
- What did you learn about life?

Regardless of the takeaway, when a person talks about pivotal seasons of life which involve pain, they demonstrate a remarkable power on that subject, which can also be used to help others.

What Are Your Power Messages?

If you're going to coach, you must discover what your power messages are. Power messages come from your own evaluated experiences and are essential tools to help you achieve your coaching objectives with a client.

Every coach has to work on universal coaching skills, tools, training, and knowledge—but they need to work equally hard to discover what is unique to them, because you want to give the client the very best version of you.

If I've taken you through our latest timeline exercise, I'd quickly begin to see patterns in how you approach life and work: your signature style. If I went back and reviewed your story, we'd probably find that something you learned in your journey was a major driver in how you operate—and a potential source of tremendous power which helps you today.

Your power messages are life lessons you've learned through your story. Experience in a certain area of life and work brings authority. Every coach needs to know their power messages and be able to use them during a coaching engagement.

"Story" is a word that normally applies to past events, but in coaching we also refer to being intentional about writing your *future* story. This is the essence of coaching: doing the work to help the client look to the future and become intentional about taking steps to get there—with the help of a coach.

Conversely, if you haven't properly recovered from a significant pain in your past, it can skew your perspective and lessen your ability to coach well.

Coaches need to have a firm grasp on their own story, in order to help someone move their story forward. It's always a powerful moment in a session when a coach is able to say, "Let me tell you what I learned when I went through a similar situation."

Those who lead themselves well are usually people who have great perspective on their life—where they've been, where they are today, and where they're going.

Your story can give you power, and your power informs your signature coaching style.

Your style and story informs who you'll be best able to coach.

You need self-leadership to identify—and stay true to—your natural coaching style.

The Laser and the Flood Light

When I (Dianne) think about coaching styles, the first area that comes to mind is how different Nathan and I are in our approaches. He's like a surgeon who goes right to the heart and starts solving problems. I'm more relational and want to know everything about the client—their family, marriage, professional life, and story. I'm also a natural encourager and love to help my clients build more belief in themselves as we move forward.

We're similar in our transparency, and willing to share what we've learned in our journey—and how we learned it. I like to help a client self-discover, but I'm also willing to share my story.

Nathan coaches like a laser, and I coach like a flood light. I want the coaching environment to be bright and warm before we do the heavy work. I want the client to feel like they are heard, and that I understand them. We almost always have the same insights, but naturally deliver them in different ways.

We both bring the light, but use different styles.

Nathan's laser-style approach to coaching works for him because the lion share of his clients are executives. They place a high value on their time and appreciate a direct approach: "Don't tell me what I *want* to hear, but rather what I *need* to hear to be successful in my leadership."

His clients love that he is laser focused, and doesn't take offense. They often thank him for his direct approach. Honestly, I used to think, *Man, you are awfully blunt.* But as I've watched him over the years I've realized, it's his natural style, and he knew exactly how to communicate in a way that client would receive it.

When I need to give a client constructive criticism, I like to use the sandwich method: start with a compliment, then provide the critique and recommendations, then end with a positive by reminding the client about areas of progress. That's my natural style.

It's natural for a new coach to want to emulate a particular style, and that's okay. Trying new approaches is one way we learn to find our authentic style. It's like trying on new shoes—they might look good on someone else, but you have to wear them yourself to make sure they're a comfortable fit.

Another way we can learn what coaching style works best is to simply ask the client.

Case Study: Can We Adjust Our Coaching Style?

Years ago a new client said to me, "Dianne, you can shoot straight with me." I can hear you better if you tell me what I need to hear in as few as words as possible.

I thought I was being direct. But I tried to adjust my delivery to better suit the way she was wired. I was still me, but a more direct version of me. How did the coaching relationship turn out? Stay tuned.

We've learned to ask clients, "How do you best receive feedback when I need to share something that may be hard for you to hear?" This question opens up important connections that help you both achieve the coaching objectives. But be aware, often a client doesn't really know what style is best for them. (That's where the Birkman® assessment is invaluable to us and our coaching team; it spells out what they need.) No matter what a new client tells you about their preferred communication style, be a keen observer of their personality—and stay true to your style.

Remember, the goal is to be awesome and deliver amazing results. To be awesome, you must stay in your lane. Let's use an automotive analogy. In a race, which is faster, a sports car with four hundred horsepower, or an SUV with two hundred horsepower? The answer depends on the race course. Around a paved track, the sports car will win. But if the race is on a rocky, dirt road the SUV will outperform on every measure.

What's the lesson here? Other than the fact that Nathan and I enjoy renting all-terrain vehicles and touring remote mountain roads, the real lesson is to know what kind of car you are, and what kind of tracks you like to drive on.

It's true that you can—and should—calibrate your interactions. But the calibration control only turns so far until it breaks.

If you move out of your signature coaching style you'll lose your power and compromise your effectiveness. Power comes from your uniqueness—which comes from your unique story and style.

How did my coaching relationship turn out? We both chose to be direct and say, "Let's just be friends." And we still are to this day. It's good to make some adjustments in communication for your clients, but stay true to your style. It's a win-win proposition.

Passionate or Practical?

We have a long history of working with Lori, and as we launched Real Coaching Success she became very interested in building a successful coaching career. Lori had been doing a very small amount of coaching on her own, has a natural coaching style, but didn't have the professional processes to help her business grow.

As she went through the training, she became one of the most proficient and effective coaches we'd seen. As a matter of fact, there were times I (Nathan) thought she was a better coach than me. Lori would ask questions in a way I never considered.

As the year progressed, she struggled to build a book of business—and it made no sense. She was professional, understood our tools backward and forward, and continually added new skills. So, we scheduled a session to dig deeper. What we discovered was a real surprise.

Lori wasn't *passionate* about coaching. But she is gifted and was intellectually connected with the practice of coaching.

"If you weren't coaching what would you really like to do?"

Without hesitation she started sharing about writing a book and public speaking around her power message. We happened to know what her power messages were, and knew this meeting marked the end of her coaching business—in its current form anyway.

"Lori you have to pursue your passion, because passion naturally assists you to become excellent in whatever you are doing. When you are *excellent,* people will want to be around you and engage with your business."

She is currently on her way to publishing her book and speaking professionally. Why would we tell you a story about someone who decided to take a path different than coaching? Because you can be really *good* at coaching skills, but your passion plays a critical role in your success.

For any coach who is struggling, the lack of referrals points to the lack of one or more of these ingredients: passion, professionalism, and skills. If you believe you have a passion for coaching, then it's time to focus on building your skills and professionalism.

Answer or Guide?

There is a philosophy in the coaching world which teaches that you never give the client the "answer." Instead, you guide them and you work together as a team to help them find the answer. Have you ever wrestled with this issue?

Well, here's our *answer*: we reject this view. Early in my career I (Nathan) tried being the silent sherpa, and it drove me bananas. I knew exactly what the guys in front of me needed to hear, and yet I watched them struggle through the mental mountains and valleys. Talk about exhausting! After a few sessions I decided to ask, in my most polite and restrained style, "Do you want me to tell you what you need to hear?"

"Yes!" they immediately blurted out—as if to say, *You're my coach. Why wouldn't you?*

To my surprise, I received a lot more praise for this approach. Clients said one of the things they appreciated the most was that I told them the truth in a direct manner. Of course when I believe there's a breakthrough the client can quickly discover, I'll ask them guiding questions. But why withhold valuable insight?

In another example, as I trained one of our coaches we reviewed two of her clients' Birkman® Report. For one client I advised, "You need to be direct with her." and for the other I recommended, "You need to build the relationship before you get too direct with him." We were both glad to learn the approached worked well with each client.

Every Successful Coach Has This Style

There's a word for a truth-teller without humility or professionalism: a jerk.

Before you deliver what you *think* the answer is, you must know the client and understand something about how they are wired. That's the professionalism component. Most importantly you must maintain a humble attitude. That's the most important style for a successful coach.

There are times in sessions when I believe I know something a client needs to hear, but I'm not sure if the time is right to share it. Sometimes I need to check myself (humility) and sometimes the client may not be ready to hear it. I may wait three sessions to share it, or I may discover that my insight was not as brilliant as it seemed.

Coaches Are Truth Tellers

At Lead Self Lead Others, our fourth core value is as follows:

We are truth tellers.
We value client discovery but we do not shy away
from telling them the truth.
We believe truth is what people are really seeking.

We coach because we love people and we are believe everyone should experience their full potential. Always bring your best insights and share the truth. And remember to always speak the truth in love. You'll never go wrong with love as your foundational coaching style.

Questions for the Coach:

What are two or three of your power messages?

_____
_____
_____
_____
_____
_____
_____
_____

How would you describe your natural coaching style?

_____
_____
_____
_____
_____
_____
_____
_____

Chapter 5
Who to Coach or Not to Coach?

A pulse and a credit card are not the only qualifications for a prospective client.

Being wise about who to coach and who not to coach is a function of self-leadership, because it takes personal vision, effort, and discipline.

The goal is to be clear about your "yes" and to have the guts to say "no."

It's not just who you want to coach. The question is, *Who are you equipped to coach, at this moment in your career?* You may dream of coaching professional athletes., but have you ever excelled in sports? Don't sell yourself short, but don't oversell yourself either.

Understanding your "no" is equally important.

No and Yes

Once a year I (Nathan) have a wonderful opportunity to lead a self-leadership workshop for about 75 people in their early twenties who are giving serious consideration to their life and career. These young people are part of a program we recommend and support. One of our sons went through the program and it changed his life.

As a way to give back, I guide them through the Birkman® process. They are one of our favorite organizations but one of my more difficult engagements. Why?

Because I struggle to connect with people in their twenties. They deserve a much more engaging presenter. Where they are in life feels like such a long time ago for me. I struggle to connect with the challenges they are facing on the journey of their twenties.

I don't want to *coach* them. But I do want to help them.

So I take a few of our certified coaches to handle the facilitation and conversations. It's great experience for the coaches—

and the young people. Every time a parent asks me to coach their college-age kid, I'm happy to connect them with one of our coaches.

This same principle of knowing when you are the best fit applies to those who want coaching, but really need something else.

Saying No to Counseling

We've never taken on a client together as a couple. But we have brought each other in when the topic merited additional perspective. We're very comfortable operating in our own lanes, with our own signature styles. And we're very clear about where coaching ends and counseling begins.

As coaches, we're focused on achieving outcomes. When someone begins to move toward their desired outcomes, internal obstacles and resistance emerges. Root issues are exposed. Life change can be messy. And disruptive. *And* deeply personal. Making changes often intersects with dynamics in a client's personal life and marriage. When those dynamics impact the client's ability to move forward, you must make the choice to address those personal issues, or not.

There is a way to *acknowledge* these issues, but not take on the role of a counselor—by making it clear to the client that it's their responsibility to dig deeper on those issues which are outside the scope of the coaching engagement and objectives. We need to help the client find their "why" and their sense of purpose—their core motivations—so they can lead themselves well. And their self-leadership will help them face the personal issues that might be holding them back.

In my (Dianne's) early coaching years, my job was to help clients build their business—and I tried to keep everything focused on business activities. But the real world isn't all business. Doing homework and moving toward goals often bumps up against personal challenges.

"Did you do the homework from last week's session?" I'd ask.

Clients who answered "no" often had very personal reasons for their lack of progress. Telling them to "try harder this week" wasn't going to cut it. (Although I tried that approach early on, because that's how I'm wired.)

At this point you can either counsel someone's personal life, or coach them toward their future story.

There's a fine line between coaching and counseling. But that line is an electric fence to us!

Some coaches can operate in both arenas, but we don't recommend coaching someone who needs counseling. You can still be their coach, but you should put the coaching on pause if they remain stuck because of unresolved issues in their past. Of course you can check in with them periodically, but in our view a coach should steer away from counseling. We also recommend for coaches to have solid referral relationships with at lease three licensed counselors.

Remember, coaching is about the future; counseling is about repairing the past and coping with the present. How do you determine when it's time to say, "Hey, I believe it's time to take a pause from coaching"? When the past dominates your coaching conversations. You may also notice that a client who needs some counseling often does not do their homework, because the homework is all about moving forward.

Your coaching power resides in helping people move their story *forward*.

Who to Coach: The Style Test

When I (Nathan) take a new or prospective client through my discovery process, I'll give them a sense of my style, based on my power message and my personality, which is direct and straightforward.

We don't use scripts, but I often present something similar to the following: (Don't try this at home!)

"Here's how this works. I'm going to pay close attention to who you are and where you want to go. And I'll give you some work to do and I expect you to do it. Can you handle that? I don't do suggestions. I'm a straight shooter. My job is to help you get there. And my style is to tell you what I see, and I have no hesitation about holding you accountable along the way. Are you okay with that?"

I want them to experience *my* particular style because if they need more of a gentle encourager, I'm probably not the best guy for them. The flip side is even better. When you allow a prospective client to sense your style and power message—and it's exactly what they're looking for—you suddenly have no competition in the coaching marketplace.

To be clear, my sample presentation is not a formula. You owe it to yourself—and your clients—to discover your unique style and power messages.

I sometimes say, "If you're stuck, I'm your guy. I'll get you *unstuck*, because I'm a pusher and this is what I do for a living." Some people need a pusher and some need a different approach. The key is to know yourself, lead yourself, and present yourself accurately and confidently. This is the beauty of our company having multiple coaches on our team, in addition to a large network of other coaches, consultants, and counselors.

You can't specialize in every kind of coaching.

Case Study: It's Not Me—it's You

Betty was late for her appointment. When we finally got down to business, she confessed that she hadn't finished her homework. This was the third week in a row she hadn't done the work.

I (Dianne) realized I continued to believe that I could help Betty in this season, even when the evidence was against us. My relational-encourager style can lend itself to what we now call "over-coaching."

In this situation, my strength and my faith in people, was working against us. My hope was ignoring reality. Our coaching sessions were enjoyable and she promised to do better by next week.

What would you do in this situation?

Case Study: What I Did

In my early years of coaching, I (Dianne) sometimes gave myself credit for client success—but I always blamed myself when a client didn't make progress.

I took failures personally because I didn't have a standard for evaluating my coaching. You can coach two people in the exact same way, and sometimes one client will thrive and the other client will stall.

Measure your performance and strive for excellence, but don't take all the credit or all the blame. And remember, there's always more happening in a client's life than we're aware of. That's why we never judge them. It may be that their current life circumstances were simply too daunting for them to engage with the work at that time. Sometimes this means it's time to end or pause the coaching relationship.

In those situations I've learned to say, "Hey, I feel like coaching is not beneficial right now, would you agree? And that's okay. I'll be here when you are ready to re-engage."

Then I have a coaching conversation with myself.

Did I bring my best?

What did I learn from this engagement?

No, Thank You

A client referred me, (Nathan) to one of his colleagues, so we set up a phone call to meet and discuss his objectives. This referral happened to be with a highly successful individual, well-known in some circles, and worked for a brand I highly respected.

After a few minutes on the phone I recognized what he needed was exactly what I was good at. He was thinking through the next ten years of his career and wanted a coach to help him make the most of his opportunities. And did I mention this client had the means to pay my highest-tier rate?

But there was a problem. For me anyway. As our discussion progressed, I began to realize I might not be the best coach for this man. One of our Lead Self Lead Others certified coaches had the personality, experience, and power message that would help this client in ways I could not.

Needless to say, I faced a very difficult decision.

After every coaching engagement we send clients a survey about their experience. We're grateful to report that each survey—and we've received thousands—reflects 100 percent satisfaction.

A few months after my phone call with this man, his survey came to my inbox. I stopped what I was doing and opened the form.

He raved about his experience being coached, which made me smile. But the coach wasn't me.

You see, I referred him to Rod, one of our certified coaches, who I suspected would do a better job with this client.

Yes, this was a tough choice, but worth it. We're in this business for the long-term and you can never go wrong by doing what you believe is best for the client.

Take Your Pulse

A successful client must have more than a pulse. Who should you coach? The answer will become clearer as you coach yourself and lead yourself well.

- Get in touch with your story.
- Clarify your power messages.
- Quantify your life experiences.
- Embrace your unique personality.
- Become more confident in presenting your style of coaching.

Based on above, articulate who needs what you have to offer.

Questions for the Coach:

Who are the people you have the most confidence in coaching?

_____
_____
_____
_____
_____
_____
_____
_____
_____
_____

Why?

_____
_____
_____
_____
_____
_____
_____
_____
_____

Chapter 6
Professionalism: What are Your Motives and Standards?

The title of Professional Coach should not be an oxymoron.

The coaching industry is—to put it mildly—unregulated.

There are two sides to the coin when it comes to this lack of accreditation and continuing education. On one side, low barriers allow anyone to enter the arena. This is wonderful for those of us who might not have the time or money to invest in professional development—and want to begin helping people as soon as possible. But others can buy business cards for twenty bucks or add "coach" to their LinkedIn profile and *voilà!* They have a coaching business card, but have no idea what they're doing.

The same reality applies to coaching certifications. Build a web site and offer to "certify" coaches—for a fee—and you're in business.

Potential clients are often confused because of the lack of standardized credentials—or jaded by those who have made a mockery of how a professional coach should operate.

Frankly, the state of the industry almost kept us from launching Real Coaching Success training and certifications. We can't change the fact that the coaching arena is a bit like the wild west, but we can do something for ourselves and the industry. We can lead by example.

Professionalism

Self-leadership is the first step toward excellence, because it puts you in a position to take the next step: developing as a true professional.

When I (Nathan) began coaching, the engagements were fun, the results were good, and referrals began to happen. Everything flowed fairly effortlessly—until it didn't.

Coaching was not difficult for me. In fact, the conversations were energizing. I was having a blast. But the more I coached, the more

I had to admit I was operating from my natural personality and limited memory.

"I've been thinking about you, and I have this book I want you to read," I said with a sage's knowing smile.

"I already read it last month, remember?" the client replied, without a smile.

"What did your wife, Jane have to say about that?" I asked.

"My wife's name is Mary."

Finally, I admitted to myself, *I cannot keep doing this. It's way beneath my standard of care. And now that I think about it, I really don't have a standard of care. I'm a professional and I must improve myself as a professional.*

I started to push myself to identify my values, practices, and standard—and began to study the mechanics of coaching. I sat down and started designing what an excellent coaching practice looks like. I wanted to take it to the next level.

And deep down, I knew my livelihood depended on it.

Your Motivations

Do you have clear motives for coaching? What about coaching standards—can you list them?

Your motives will inform your standards—or lack thereof. And your standards will reveal your motives.

Our daily mission for ourselves and our team is: we coach people to help them move their stories forward and experience their full potential. What's your mission? And is your mission clear, consistent, and compelling?

Effective leaders have a clear, teachable leadership point of view and are willing to share it with and teach it to others.[10]

Success commonly means using your knowledge and experience to satisfy yourself with fame and fortune. Significance, however, means using the same knowledge and experience to serve others—that is, to change lives.[11]

---

[10] Summary of research by Noel Tichy quoted in *Helping People Win at Work* Blanchard/Ridge, p.67
[11] *Finishing Well*, Bob Buford, p.25

You need a coaching vision.[12]

One Size Does Not Fit All

One of the distinctive characteristics we decided upon went against the current of what we saw in the coaching industry. Instead of guiding clients through our "plan"—or template—we would create custom coaching tracks for each and every client.

If you think this approach might create a huge amount of extra work—from proposal to follow-up—you're correct. If you wonder if it's worth it, let me also confirm that it is.

There is some value in pre-programed coaching, just as there's value in training wheels on a child's bike. But you want to reach your full potential, don't you?

What makes this custom approach workable is your toolbox. When an electrician arrives at an appointment, they might not know much about the situation and how to address it, but they do have a truckload of proven tools for the job.

In the beginning, we had one tool. You can turn a bolt with a pair of pliers, but it doesn't take long to figure out that a wrench works much better. So we added tools based on what clients needed. Professional coaches have tools, and they use those tools in a customized plan.

How Long Is a Coaching Engagement?

Part of any customized plan is the *planned timeline* of a coaching engagement. It is a bit of an uncertainty in the beginning of a relationship as to how long it will take to achieve the coaching objectives, but clients deserve to know what they are entering into. Many aspiring coaches assume that a successful coaching relationship should go on forever. Or until the client fires you.

Not a great way to operate a coaching business. It is better to begin with the end in mind and accept the reality that the relationship is temporary.

---

[12] How Will You Measure Your Life? by Clayton M. Christensen. Reprint R1007B

Especially for those starting a coaching practice, the prospecting of a pre-determined period can be a bit scary. *Why talk about ending the engagement before we even begin?*

Two answers:

1) Because a timeline will help you and the client focus on achieving objectives
2) Being up front about the proposed timeline can actually help a potential client feel more comfortable about committing to a certain time period

We always include a recommended "duration"—the word we use in our proposals. If the timeline is "forever" you're not coaching, you're a professional best friend. *So, what happens when the time period ends?*

I (Nathan) have coached a client for eight years, but we constantly renew our coaching objectives. For example, I work with him for four months, and on a certain date we review the goals. We celebrate our wins, and if we find other areas he wants to address, we continue for another period of time. The relationship can also shift to where I become a "trusted advisor," available as needed versus the typical coaching relationship.

Some clients tell me, "I need a few months to work on what we've covered." It's not uncommon for clients to re-engage after a pause of a month—or after two or three years. It's important to note that some coaching engagements morph into the role of being a personal advisor and that is why a client may extend beyond the typical duration.

Re-engagement comes from results. Referrals come from results. That's why results are always the goal.

We realize that "pre-firing" a client can seem daunting, and can create tension in a coaching business. Welcome to business! When you get nervous about this, or any other aspect of coaching, go back to your *motives* for coaching. A successful coaching business is built on referrals, which is built on success. Locking in "contracts" is not the goal, creating success stories is the goal.

By the way, we don't use contracts for coaching. Why? I want clients to be able to fire me with a text. And I want to deliver excellence. Does a formal, signed agreement really change the business relationship? Will you sue a client if they stop showing up to appointments? Of course not. But many of our coaches and strategic partners choose to use contracts.

We do use agreements for *consulting* projects, because some clients are businesses or nonprofit corporations which rightly expect us to provide detailed deliverables and terms.

We're in business to help people. The clients—and the money—will follow.

Write It Down to Follow Up

Every workday morning, I carefully review every upcoming appointment by concentrating on what I know about the client, where they've been in the engagement, and where we want to go in our meeting to meet our objectives. I also review notes from previous sessions.

How do I make sure that when the client arrives, I'm ready to deliver 200 percent?

Preparation and follow-up are a continuing cycle. You need to prepare in order to have an excellent coaching session, and you need helpful notes to prepare. We'll examine the art of note-taking soon, but here's the takeaway: preparation is key to professionalism.

Follow-up

For many months, my follow-up consisted of a parting, "I'll see you next week!" I believed I gave the client everything they needed to move their story forward until our next meeting. And we've since learned that countless coaches operate this way.

During the course of an engagement, I realized I needed to crystalize some helpful thoughts and resources—and send a follow-up email to the client within 24 hours. I hoped the follow-up would help the client re-focus and stay focused until our next meeting. And it did. Clients rave about it.

This standard creates two challenges: good note-taking skills during a session and the discipline to email follow-up information within one day. But the practice also helped me stay more focused on holding the client accountable. (It also eliminated the embarrassing "You already asked me to read that article" moments.)

When I started to improve as a coach, I was able to up my level of professionalism. I became much more skilled at moving a client forward. The follow-up email is a central part of our system.

If you have five coaching sessions today, by the time you've finished four appointments, you'll barely remember what you spoke about in your first two sessions—let alone what you covered in yesterday's meetings. You have a choice: either keep trying to do the impossible (and sabotage your business) or increase your capacity with professionalism.

We recommend trying to end each session at the forty-five-minute mark. Schedule at least 30 minutes in between each session to finish notes, recharge, and prepare for the next client.

Because my (Nathan) natural style of coaching is to be direct, I have had to learn to be holistically direct when I write my follow-up emails to my clients. Not only do I need to be direct about their next steps to move forward, but also be direct about where I see progress and how I feel about their efforts. Because my direct style sometimes doesn't translate well in emails, I've learned to be more intentional about offering encouragement and affirmation about the progress I see. Instead of simply sending a few bullet points, I'll reflect on what might genuinely motivate the client to lead themselves well.

Case Study: Professionalism Over Pizzazz

Three years into my full-time career as a coach, a CEO I'd never met asked his HR leader to get an executive coaching quote from two companies: a well-established firm with several coaches . . . and me. After a brief meeting with the executive, it was time to create a proposal. Problem was, I'd never written a proposal before.

Lead Self Lead Others had no template, so I simply did my best to present what I saw, and how we could help. The document was one page but represented hours of work.

I attached the PDF to an email, took a deep breath, and hit send.

Professionalism Sets You Apart

"Everybody—and their dog—seems to be a coach these days. How can I compete?"

We say, the more people who coach the better, because most won't do it well and it helps our company stand out. Yes, competition creates noise. But your ideal clients can probably hear through the coaching noise because they're looking for a true professional. As with other professions, those who over-deliver can build a business based on referrals.

We think it is fair to criticize coaches who are likely to hold coaches in disregard. Counselors often believe many coaching clients should be in their counseling chair. As you build a network of counselors you can refer people to, you'll show them how you respect the line between coaching and counseling. And HR professionals are in the people business, and also have continuing education requirements and standards. But if you can demonstrate to a human resources director how you fill an important role, they can become a referral gold mine—especially if they work in a big company.

Our company has the honor of being a resource for 35 senior partners in a CPA firm with 350 employees. This engagement came from their head of HR, who saw the need, but also recognized he did not have the skills to help their senior leaders develop workplace relationships and leadership skills. (The funny thing about many surgeons, engineers, and CPAs is they often can't get along with each other very well. Because they're naturally oriented toward *task* expertise, and don't always have the best communication skills, so conflicts tends to arise.)

These people need coaches who are true professionals.

Professionals Have a Mission

A professional coach must be able to articulate why they coach and the values by which they operate.

Here are our basic core values at Lead Self Lead Others:
- We create custom coaching and consulting plans for our clients
- We manage time well

- We calibrate our coaching to fit the uniqueness of our clients
- We are truth tellers
- We engage in ongoing training, development, and evaluation of our coaching and consulting skills.
- We offer our own lives as examples of people who lead themselves well.

> The full list can be found in the Appendix or at http//:LeadSelfLeadOthers.com.

Case Study: The One Page Proposal

The next day, the reply hit my inbox. "We've decided to go with your company, Nathan."

In our first in person meeting, the executive confided, "The reason you won the job is because you listened to me, and your proposal reflected that fact." He then showed me the other proposal which was very generic—it could have been sent to almost any other CEO. Because I'd been doing my homework on active listening, I used my note-taking skills in our initial meeting. The result was a completely customized proposal that addressed his needs and goals.

We are very serious about customization in everything we do. We're all about the client, including the proposal we submit. If it takes two hours to craft a professional proposal, that's what we do. Of course, we've developed some formats and verbiage to help speed the process from a blank page. But the end result is never cookie-cutter.

We go deep into the process of creating excellent proposals in Real Coaching Success training and certification, but here's the bottom line: interview the potential client and really listen, then translate what you heard from them into your proposal. You'd expect the same level of professionalism from an attorney or physician. Why do we expect less of coaches?

Professionalism makes you money. Professionalism adds a zero to your coaching income.

Questions for the Coach:

Who is the most professional person you know?

What is it about them that impresses you?

What are some way that you can become more professional in your coaching?

_____
_____
_____
_____
_____
_____
_____
_____
_____
_____

Chapter 7
Professionalism: Do You Have Clear Coaching Objectives?

Coaching a bunch of clients sounds like a great idea, until you try it.

Coaching objectives are what a coach uses to move a person's story forward.

If you are coaching one or two people, you can probably get by with having all the information about your clients in your head. But beyond that, you need to discipline yourself and have written coaching objectives for each person you are working with. As stated earlier, it is critical that you are crystal clear about *why* you are coaching each client.

And before you can help a client establish their objectives, you must be clear about your own professional objectives.

Coaching Objectives for your Client

In our proposals, the very first element we include is our understanding of the current objectives for the coaching engagement. (We also include our *process*, the *duration*, the *investment*, and more.) In our experience, most coaches don't even do the work to determine a clear goal before the coaching begins, and as a result, never establish it during the process.

But if you've had even one client, and had an objective, you know that it's a challenge to stay focused on the goal. In coaching, you never know what topic will come up. Do you chase all those rabbits or do you stick to the stated purpose of the engagement? We'd answer that you must do both.

First, never lose sight of—and never hesitate to remind your client about—your agreed upon goals. That said, if you agree the formal objective needs to change, then change it and stick with the new objective.

The stated—and written—outcome of your coaching must be front and center in your mind, in your notes, in your follow-up, and in your coaching. In fact, we know the coaching objectives of every client our team coaches because their proposals are kept in a file.

Chasing Rabbits

Exercises can be interesting. Timelines can open up endless discussions. Even an assessment, like the Birkman®, can open up dozens of potential rabbit trails. It's possible for a coach to become obsessed with assessments.

Self-discovery is a lifetime process—but coaching should not be.

You could have 52 coaching sessions in order to understand your client's particular personality and needs. But that's not the goal. In the end—and this is a profound point—the *goal* is the goal.

From a coaching standpoint, helping your client achieve their objective is the highest priority. Yes, it will be difficult at times to shift the trajectory of a session toward the stated goals, but it's always worth it. *Results* are what we're after.

From a business standpoint, results produce referrals. And referrals are the only path to real coaching success.

Who is responsible to establish agreed upon objectives? You are.

Who is responsible to steer the coaching sessions back to the objectives? You are.

Listening for Understanding for Objectives

One key to real coaching success is *to listen to understand*. And this process starts before the prospect becomes a client. But we're not simply talking about the passive reception of sound waves—a coach needs to be an *active* listener. This kind of listening requires intentional effort.

- Processing what the client is saying.
- Asking follow-up questions.
- Looking for consistent threads—or inconsistencies.
- Watching for dramatic expression.

- Being alert for new information.
- Skillfully interrupting to ask questions.

Most of all, the goal is to achieve understanding. If you're not sure what the client is trying to convey, you must ask, "What did you mean by that?"

One of my favorite things to do in a meeting is to say something along the lines of, "Fred, do you realize you've said 'darn' five times since we sat down? What's up with that?" I'm listening for patterns and departure from norms. When I give a client a sincere compliment and they wince, or shrug it off, I like to pause and ask about their reaction—because it shows that I'm paying attention. But the real purpose is to help the client go deeper, so we can reach their objectives.

"This is what I hear you saying . . . Does that sound right?"

Active listening is like wrestling. When I (Nathan) wrestled in high school, my hands were always up. Prepared for any move my opponent might make. In coaching, I'm always leaning in—dialed in to what the client is saying so I *understand* the client.

I'm looking for anything that is holding the client back from what we've identified as their objective. I'm always listening for insights—to remove barriers to their progress and steer the client toward their full potential.

We had a client who worked ridiculously-long hours and was grumpy. During our meetings I realized he didn't really need to be at the office that much, which revealed the root issue. He didn't need coaching for goal setting or time management. And he wasn't grumpy because of his work schedule. What he really needed was to work on his personal relationships.

In conversations with prospective clients, we listen for what might be their true objective. Sometimes they have a clear understanding of what they want and sometimes they don't. They just know they want help. But always ask questions to see if what they *say* they're looking for in a coaching relationship is the result they really want.

You must have a great *discovery* conversation with potential clients in order to identify the "coaching gap" and the objectives that will close the gap between where they are and where they want to be. If you obtain enough information from the conversation, then schedule another one. My all-time record for number of discovery conversations is three. I was struggling to find the clarity I knew I needed to identify the coaching gap. Finally, during the third conversation I asked the right question and the light bulb appeared. The client commented later how he was very impressed with my commitment to find the right objective before we even began coaching sessions. (And in this case, the discovery conversations were offered at no cost to him.)

Distilling the best coaching objectives is an art and a science—and something we cover in detail in our training, workshops, and certification. But no matter your level of experience, the concept of establishing clear goals is something you can put into practice immediately. And it does require practice.

Objectives Before, During, and After the Session

We don't charge by the hour. Many times coaches work more hours for our clients before and after the session than *in* the session.

The key to results (which generate referrals) is to focus on the stated goals—before, during, and after the session. It's crucial to keep the coaching objectives as your top priority as you prepare and follow up with your clients.

I'm surprised at how quickly I (Nathan) can forget a coaching objective. For as long as I've been in the coaching business, I've needed to discipline myself in this area, so I know other coaches also need to.

I need to continually review the why. *Why exactly am I meeting with this client today?*

We begin our preparation by reviewing past notes—and at the top of my notes is the objective. I often write it out in big letters and draw a circle around it. I re-answer the question: *Why is the client coming to see me?*

Many clients have a strong personality, and can easily veer off from the core issues. If you don't keep the clear objective in mind, the session will fly by without making true progress.

Remember, *you* are responsible to prepare for the session with a solid grasp of the stated objectives.

After the session, I review my notes, but in the context of the objective. Client discussions rarely follow a straight line, and many intriguing opportunities for conversations will emerge. But I ask myself, *Does this line of follow-up help us achieve the purpose of our coaching engagement?*

In the follow-up email, I'll sometimes re-state our objective, in order to put the assignments in context. When clients connect the dots between work and the goal, motivation multiplies. (As you can already see, the follow-up email not only helps the client, but helps you to stay focused, and helps you prepare for the next session. It's a win-win-win.)

You are responsible to make sure the follow-up stays on course.

Objectives Cut Through the Fog

There are objectives for the coaching engagement as a whole, but there can also be objectives for a particular session or time period between sessions.

Sometimes the longer-term objective can be clear, but the next step to get there can seem foggy. In those situations we've learned to cut through the fog by asking the client a question about a question.

"Based on what we've covered today, what fog cutting question should I ask you when we sit down together next week?"

We let the client come up with the questions. Sometimes they are able to in the moment and at other times they need to think about it and just email or text. Because client can see what obstacles they face and where they need accountability. (The question they provide is often quite revealing as well.) The question becomes the objective for the upcoming week and sets the agenda in the client's mind. We have found that teaching a client how to use fog cutting questions is something they continue to do on their own after the coaching engagement comes to a conclusion.

Post-engagement: Did We Hit the Objectives?

You already know we survey every client when an engagement ends. (Contact us to learn more about the Client Experience Survey and other resources.) When we and our coaches review the questionnaire, we're on the lookout for three main areas:

- What can we learn to improve as a coach and a company?
- Does the client believe the objective was achieved?
- Will they refer us to others?

If there was no clear goal, the client's response is subjective. But when all parties agree to the coaching objectives, the review requires zero rocket science. The coach knows if they delivered, and so does the client. And the clients who experience results make referrals.

Questions for the Coach:

What questions would be most helpful to you to understand your clients coaching experience with you?

_____
_____
_____
_____
_____
_____
_____
_____
_____

Which questions might feel a little intimidating to ask? (Hint: These are probably the ones to ask.)

_____
_____
_____
_____
_____
_____
_____
_____
_____

Chapter 8
Professionalism: Coaching Skills for Real Success

Your personality and excitement can help you get started, but your skills determine your success.

A successful coach should be excited about their work. But excitement won't create results.

One of the coaches we trained was very passionate about helping her clients and the energy was very present in her client sessions. (We know this because new coaches sometimes ask us to be present in a session or listen to a recording of the session, with client consent.) This coach was so excited she couldn't seem to refrain from interrupting her client when they tried to respond.

We knew immediately that the next portion of her training would focus on improving her emotional intelligence.[13] In particular, the third metric that goes into producing her emotional quotient score. It's one thing to be self-aware, it's another thing to be aware of how you are affecting the other person. Frankly, despite her intentions, she wasn't aware the client was becoming agitated.

The key to talking with a client is to know what to say and when to say it and how to say it. If your timing is off, or if you rush the client, you won't have the same impact. Just because you have the "answer" doesn't mean you have to say it at that moment. Coaches need to deliver the right answer at the right time. Every time she interrupted the client, he became more and more frustrated and ignored her repeatedly saying, "I'm sorry. I interrupted you. Go ahead." She was not aware that every time she cut the client off, it was frustrating the client.

The rhythm of the client's responses changed. He was very forthcoming at first, then he started slowing down on his answers. He

---

[13] https://www.amazon.com/dp/0974320625/

became more hesitant and guarded because he didn't believe the coach was truly listening and understanding him.

But she had no clue—because she was focusing on meeting *her* needs instead of the needs of the client.

After the call, I interviewed the coach and asked, "How do you think your session went?"

"Fantastic!" she immediately replied.

"For who?" I asked.

"What do you mean?"

"It was fantastic for you, but not so much for the client. Do you know why?"

After a long pause and a shrug, I answered, "Because you have a habit of interrupting. You need to be aware and change, or you will never reach your full potential as a great coach."

So we went to work on her emotional intelligence score. By the way, the great news about emotional intelligence is that you can improve in every aspect. To serve our clients better, we must develop better skills. This takes time and effort.

Your skills—not your personality or natural abilities—determine your success.

How do you know if you're "coasting" on your personality? It's simple. If you can't list the action you're taking and the time you're investing to build your skills every week or month, you're coasting. Whether you feel like it or not. In the next section we'll review a few skills crucial for real coaching success.

The best coaches we work with are the ones who continually study their craft so they consistently deliver excellence.

Understanding

Having good listening skills does not necessarily make you a good coach. You must also be skilled in understanding.

A technique we use, as a mental picture, is the concept of letting all the air out of an inflated balloon. The client is the balloon, and their thoughts are the air. The more I can help a client let all their air out, the more material I have to work with. The key is doing what you can as a coach to make sure they've expressed all their air and not assume you understand everything after their first sentence.

Another way we train on this topic is with the concept of winning a hand of poker. And you'll win every time if you focus on one area: have the client show you their cards. If the client shows you their cards, you'll know exactly what to do next. The more genuinely curious you are, the more you'll understand the client—and understand how to help them move forward. And this professional curiosity is expressed through questions.

"Hold on a second, let me ask you about that."

Or, "Can I repeat back what I hear you saying?"

You don't have to believe the client or agree with them, but you must work to understand them. The skill of listening to understand also builds trust in the coach client relationship.

When the situation calls for it, one of my favorite ways to formally begin a follow-up session with a client is to say, "The last time we met, you said . . . Tell me more about what you meant by that." To be able to do this, you have to recognize that although you heard the words your client said you were clear on what they *meant*. You have to be on your toes so you can ask for further clarification. Listen—*and understand—how* the statement had significant meaning, and add it to your notes.

The goal is not necessarily what a client says, the goal is to understand what they mean. You have to move past the words to the *meaning* behind the words. Then this clarity arrives, coaching becomes much easier. But you need skills to discern true understanding.

Some clients struggle to communicate because not everyone is a good communicator—especially when talking about themselves. Some people have been hurt when they've been transparent in the past, and you, as the coach, are still a stranger.

Questions like, "How does this relate to the objective we agreed to reach?" can actually help the client know your focus is on the goal, and you only have their best interests in mind. (And this is another reason why clear coaching objectives are so important.)

Speaking of focusing on the client's best interests—when you're actively listening, be sure you're not distracting them with your personality quirks. For example, imagine we're meeting with each other at a coffee shop and you're answering a question. As I'm looking you in the eye, I begin to wave my hands around. (We all know people who talk with their hands and it can be a bit distracting.)

You'd become quite annoyed, right? Your focus would shift from your answer to trying to figure out why I'm waving my hands.

That's a dramatic example, but the fact is many coaches "listen" in a distracting way.

Everything from interrupting, to how a coach takes notes (or doesn't take notes), or their facial expressions creates unnecessary distractions for the client—which creates communication barriers. Another classic growth point for a coach is to be able to adjust their pace of speaking. When some coaches are excited, they talk too fast, or too much.

Going back to the poker analogy, a coach must work on their "poker face." Remember, the goal is for the client to show you their cards. But unlike in the game of poker, you want to help *them* win.

Listening skills create understanding—which creates trust and transparency, which helps you help the client.

Characteristics of real understanding:

- I relate to where you are coming from.
- I get your world.
- I feel your tension.
- Goal: Your client says to themselves, *This coach listens, cares, and understands me.*

Observing

As with listening, observing your client is a skill that can improve with time and discipline. Human beings are natural observers, but the skill of insightful observation is a necessity for a successful coach. Of course, in person meetings provide the best opportunity to pay attention to nonverbal communication, but video calls can also be very helpful—especially early in the coaching relationship.

Let's begin with how we make an observation about a client's clothing. Yes, because we choose our clothing, we, as coaches can sometimes learn something important about a client from their wardrobe. Of course, we're not making *judgments* about a person because of what they wear, or their hair style, but a coach can sometimes find facets of a client's personality or state of mind by observing their choice of clothing or hairstyle that they might not reveal verbally.

Here are a few examples:

- Does the client leave their jacket on when they sit down?
- If they do take off their jacket, where, and how, do they place it?
- Do they *ask* for something to drink? Or do they *bring* something to drink?
- Do they frequently forget to bring their pen or notepad?
- How often do they check their phones during a session?
- Are their clothes "boring" or loud or a mix of both? (We're always interested in a person's choice of footwear and socks.) Do they have a particular "style"?
- For phone or videos calls, how do to they answer—or enter—calls? How comfortable are they with technology? What question do they usually ask you in the first five minutes of connecting with them.
- Do they arrive on time or late?

Coaching involves professional curiosity because we care about helping the client move forward. A successful coach looks for clues about a client's unique personality.

If I know a client just returned from vacation, I like to ask where they went. But this is just step one, and their answer probably won't tell you much about them. Then I'll ask *why* they chose to vacation there, what they did, and so on.

You can learn a lot about someone from watching their eye movement, especially when you ask certain questions. Do they stay focused on you? Do they look up or down or sideways? Do they take a long blink.

After a few sessions, you may find a client has a certain reflex (or "tell" in poker vernacular) when they're asked about an area of struggle or pain.

When I make a mental note of it, I'll look for the same reaction in the next session. I can tell when a client is struggling because they always look away when asked a particular question.

Again, we're skilled observers, not judges—and certainly not psychiatrists. We want to do an amazing job of coaching, and part of our job is to learn about the person in front of us. As with listening, the goal of observing is to gain deeper understanding.

Realize your observations have limitations so hold off on the interpretations.

An "expert" in body language might conclude that when a person crosses their arms or shifts in their seat, they are upset. But maybe their shoulder hurts or the chair is uncomfortable.

Focused observation is another way to get your mind off yourself and onto the client.

Truth-telling

Every coach I know would consider themselves to be truthful. But telling the truth to a client requires some skill. At Lead Self Lead Others, truth-telling means saying *what* they need to hear, *when* they need to hear it, and *how* they need to hear it.

Truth-telling is a powerful tool when the coach tells the client something they need to hear that is *pertinent to the coaching objectives*. It's an awesome experience to deliver the right truth at the right time in the right way. Have you ever seen an NFL running back take the ball and charge toward his offensive line too quickly? Sometimes he hits a wall and loses ground. But sometimes he pivots, or hesitates for a split second, and a hole opens up in the defense—and touchdown!

That's what it's like to be a skilled truth-teller.

You might have a valuable nugget of truth, but is the client ready? We recommend pausing to ponder the right time. *Right now? At the end of the session? Write it in the notes for consideration in our next session?*

One thing is certain, it's never a mistake to take a breath and consider . . . timing. It's all about helping the client move forward, and we want a high level of receptivity from the client.

We often see past clients at the grocery store or in a restaurant, and many will repeat a line we delivered to them which made a big impact. Sometimes it's a nugget of truth we delivered several years ago which stuck with them and still encourages them to move forward today.

A truth delivered at the right time sticks for a long time.

It's possible to deliver a truth at the right time, but in the wrong way for a particular client to receive it. Here again, the Birkman® takes so much guesswork out of communication. For example, if a client's report shows they have a very high need for respect, *how* I deliver the truth can make all the difference.

"Joe, I need to tell you something. And I'm only saying this because I *respect* you. I really enjoy working with you and believe in what you're doing. But here's something you need to hear."

The defenses drop, I carry the ball to the end zone, and the client wins!

I (Nathan) am naturally direct in my communication. But I need to be direct about *more* than just the nugget of truth. I've also learned to be direct about my appreciation, respect, and the fact that the truth might be difficult to hear.

I once told a new client, "One problem I see is that you don't take care of yourself and you're mad at the world. But the good news is we can do something about it, and I'll help you."

That statement was direct, but I wasn't kicking him to the curb, I was ready and willing to help. It's not necessarily the tone, it's the *attitude*. We want the client to experience our attitude about the truth— "I'm not judging you, I don't think less of you, but you need to consider this . . . "

Some clients take the truth with silence. Others process it verbally. There's no right or wrong way for a client to digest, but let them digest.

Another technique we sometimes incorporate involves saying, "Earlier, I told you this. What do you think about that? How are you doing with that statement? I know it wasn't the easiest thing to hear, so how are you feeling about it now?"

A truth is important enough to not merely *hope* the point has been made. There has to be buy-in on both sides of the coaching relationship.

The examples we've been referencing are "negative" truths that can be difficult to face. But don't overlook sharing affirming truths.

- "You've been wonderfully made."
- "This is who you are. So I want to encourage you to be this guy! *This* is the guy we are looking for!"

Those can be pretty terrific moments in the coaching relationship.

For a coach, truth-telling is a measure of the coach's maturity and emotional intelligence. When you lack the skill to deliver the truth at the right time and in the right way, you lack *skills*. When you lack the courage to tell the client a truth, you're being selfish. You're protecting yourself because you are afraid of their reaction. And you just violated Coaching 101 because it's about the client, not about you.

It takes wisdom and skill to deliver a hard truth. And it's good to pause and check the timing. But you still have to deliver the goods. That's your job.

Taking Notes

In a coaching session, we usually take very few notes. But what we write down is important—and tied to the coaching objectives.

One of our training exercises for new coaches involves having them use only one 3×5 card for notes. New coaches often veer into trying to transcribe the entire session. When that happens, they have nothing of real importance because they've written down *everything*. The key is to only write down crucial insights to help a client move toward their objectives.

My (Nathan's) notes have four sections and I use pen and paper. (Gadgets create distractions.)

First I place the client's name and date on the paper because you'd be surprised how easy it is to get client notes mixed up.

Second, I add any bio information I find interesting that I've discovered during the session. If the client mentions they attended a certain university, or they love to boat, or something unique to them, I write that down.

Third, I write down anything related to helping the client take their next step. If I'm listening to the client and don't want to interrupt their thought, I'll make a note.

Fourth, I note items I need to do for the client. For example, if I need to make a phone call for them, or send a resource to them.

That's all I write down. And I never write anything down I would not show the client if he asks. (And some clients will ask!) When I prepare the follow-up email, the important aspects are clearly written in my notes.

Coaches Are Researchers and Pathfinders

Engaged clients usually want to know, "What are my next steps?"

Moving your story forward takes steps. Next Steps Exercises are strategic activities to move the client toward the coaching objectives, which takes them toward their potential. When you've built a robust toolbox, it's really fun to say, "I have a great exercise to help you with that!"

Our follow-up emails always contain at least one Next Step Exercise.

Many coaches we train ask, "How do you come up with all this stuff for your clients to do?" They think we're walking encyclopedias, but we're simply diligent reviewers. We review our notes and take time to think about the clients. I'm sure we have over two hundred resources, PDFs, articles, podcasts, and videos in our tool box. Birkman® also offers dozens of specialized reports that target areas of interest for the client.

Our job is to help the client move forward. If we see where a client is stuck but don't know what would help them get unstuck, we have to go to work and find a solution. One of the amazing privileges of having a team of coaches at Lead Self Lead Others, is we are constantly resourcing one another.

Questions for the Coach:

Are my coaching skills up to par?

Do my coaching skills deliver with excellence?

On a scale of 1 to 10, how do I rate myself on the following skills:

Listening to understand:_____

Observing the client: _____

Truth-telling: _____

Taking notes: _____

Research for my client: _____

Follow-up with my client: _____

Chapter 9
Professionalism: Calibrate and Re-Calibrate for Real Success

A successful coach calibrates their interactions, because every client is unique.

"You're unique, just like everybody else." Yes, that line always makes me laugh. But successful coaches are serious about selecting the right tools and customized approaches to fit their clients' needs. We call this calibration.

There are many personality assessments on the market, and through the use of assessments you can understand quite a bit about the natural personality of your client—in a very short amount of time. The Birkman® Assessment instantly highlights four critical data points of a client: what they are interested in, their strengths, their hidden needs, and their stress behaviors. When you know these aspects of a client's personality, you can calibrate the coaching experience for them, but still operate in your unique coaching style.

Here's a simplified example of calibration. If I know a person tends to be task oriented, I can intentionally focus more on action items and a measured pace in our sessions. On the opposite end of the continuum, if a client is more oriented toward people and relationships, it can be helpful to slow down the coaching tasks and make sure we focus on the personal connection—particularly in the beginning. Having a high or low "literary" score will influence the amount of assigned reading.

You can find ways to learn about your clients without a formal assessment, but we've found that the process takes longer and is more prone to misunderstandings. Let's face it; it's guessing. Asking the client about their needs and stressors is a fine idea, but most people can't articulate them, or may be unwilling to open up in the first session or two. Ask any client if they want you to be direct or not, every one will tell you to shoot straight. But for half of them, that approach will backfire.

When you coach fifteen people per week, there's no way you can accurately calibrate your interactions without some help. Clients expect results—and rightly so. Taking twelve sessions to "figure out" a client might be fun for you, but it won't be for the client.

The Platinum Rule

You've heard of the Golden Rule: Treat others the way you would like to be treated. Well, we can't argue with that. But when it comes to real coaching success, we use the Platinum Rule: Treat people the way *they* prefer to be treated.

The golden rule is more about character and values and operates on the assumption the that client operates like you do. The Platinum Rule is more about platforming the client and adjusting your coaching around the client's unique personality and needs. This is the essence of calibration. To calibrate means to assess and adjust in order to operate successfully. Without using an assessment tool, making adjustments is much more difficult and won't be effective.

Musicians in an orchestra must "tune" their instruments to the same standard in order to work together in harmony, and a coach must tune into the same frequency as their client. This also relates to the third and fourth measurement of emotional intelligence: developing your awareness of how you come across to others and having the ability to make adjustments.

The more your self-awareness grows—largely based on understanding your own assessments—the more you'll be able to know how your natural style will come across to a particular client, and then you can intentionally decide how to best serve the client.

Calibration is based on the client's personality and needs. We can receive crucially-helpful insights through assessments, then adjust based on those insights. Better communication, more trust, and coaching objectives met—in less time—if you do your homework.

If you were in the room with us for five different coaching sessions, you'd see us coach in five slightly different ways. We don't become five different people or change our coaching styles. But, because we are professionals, we follow the Platinum Rule.

If I coach my clients the way *I* want to be coached, results become much more difficult to achieve. Most of your clients are not like you. When their needs are not met, frustration grows. And frustration is kryptonite to a coaching relationship—and every other kind of relationship.

For example, if a client has a high need for a democratic approach, I can still be direct, but I'll aim for direct agreement. Instead of, "Here's what you need to do . . . " I can say, "Do you think this would be good for you?"

This, and a dozen other considerate communication choices, can make or break a session. We refer to these as "client hacks."

Remember, we're not just making candles. We have the privilege of helping people live their one and only life to the fullest. If calibration helps more people move their story forward, why wouldn't we take the time and effort to pursue the best route of calibration?

We're trying to help the client alter their thinking and/or their behavior. They must trust us because we are asking them to do something they struggle with, can't do, don't want to do, or haven't done.

Helping someone get unstuck requires calibration.

Is Calibration Manipulation?

You might wonder, "Okay, Nathan and Dianne. Isn't this manipulating the client?"

And we would answer, "That's exactly what we're doing."

The word "manipulation" has a bad reputation because it's often used to describe someone pressuring another toward the manipulator's goal. (Certain negative stereotypes about salespeople come to mind.) In the end, the other person ends up feeling wronged or taken advantage of.

A musician *manipulates* the tuning keys of their instrument in order to play well with others. Mechanics use tools and operations manuals to *manipulate* machinery so it operates at its potential. (An assessment is a form of an operations manual for the client.)

If you have good coaching motives, and agreed upon objectives, making adjustment to help the client reach their potential is a pure form of service. Again, it's all about the client. Calibration is about being fully you—but without the unnecessary distractions that can derail a relationship.

I (Nathan) find entertainment value in telling stories. It's fun—for me anyway. If I take three precious minutes to tell a great story, I'll have a good time, but the client might wonder what it had to do with their goals.

The Platinum Rule rules.

Calibrating Your Energy

Coaches get tired.

Really successful coaches can get really tired.

Laser-focus requires tremendous amounts of energy. When we're tired, our concentration drifts. Our body language slurs. Our reactions slow. Our faces glaze. You're getting sleepy just reading this, aren't you?

When this happens, clients notice—either consciously or subconsciously. But they know. We might stop interjecting with questions in order to dig deeper. And you know.

So, what do we do?

You have to find the way you re-up your energy. It's a conscious decision and a skill and a discipline. We won't tell you how, but you need to find what works for you.

Maybe you need to get more sleep or exercise. You might need to change your schedule, or work with fewer clients, to deliver the results that build your business with referrals. For example, I (Dianne) have discovered that I do best when I increase the variety of locations from which I coach, as compared with staying at the same location for each coaching session. This can include simply moving to different locations around the house.

I (Nathan) have discovered that in order to stay sharp, I need 30 minutes minimum between sessions. And during these breaks, I crank up a wide variety of music.

You have to own your self-leadership to deliver excellence. You have amazing potential, but to reach it takes effort. As an example, here's an exercise you can try right now. Ready?

Raise up one hand as high as you can, straight up over your head.

(Yes, do it. Right now.)

Good.

Now raise your hand just a *little* higher.

Even though I asked you to raise your hand and "as high as you can," you could do a little bit more. Are you surprised? Sure, this exercise is a little corny, but the point is important. Raising your energy level for clients is what makes the difference between failure and success.

Managing Your Personal Dynamic

When you step into a room, the room is no longer the same.

There is a dynamic you bring, even if you don't say a word. This is another reason to practice calibration, in order to understand the dynamic you bring to a coaching session. Being mindful of your personal dynamic is just as important in a phone call or video conferencing session as it is in person.

What's the volume and tone of your voice? Is the camera angle or lighting distracting?

Am I over-reacting to the discussion, or under-reacting? (Is your reaction a distraction?) If you have a rather calm personality and the client tells you something quite meaningful you might care a lot about what's been said, but did you let your face show it?

We never record our coaching sessions. But that's mostly because I (Nathan) can't stand hearing myself talk. (Honestly, when I listened to recorded workshops I only heard what I *should have* said, and my confidence tanked.) But you might consider recording a session, with the client's permission, in order to hear yourself coach. In fact, I dare you.

The goal of listening to yourself can simply be to ask, *Where did my personal dynamic become a possible distraction to the client?*

Calibrating Your Words

A famous king said, "A truly wise person uses few words."[14]

Can you answer the question, "What's it like to hear me talk in a coaching session?" Or, "What's it like to experience the *timing* of when I ask a question or say something?

Timing is one of the most under-valued disciplines for a coach. We've come to enjoy the discipline of *not* using a ton of words in a session. Instead, we try to make sure our words are very strategic, because we want the client to remember certain things.

We also like . . . the dramatic pause.

You never know when you will say something that is an "arrow"—words that hit the bullseye at the perfect time. It's always after the session when we realize the significance of the impact. So we're disciplined, but don't overthink it.

We encourage our coaches to pay close attention to how their clients answer the following question: "What were your main takeaways from our last session?" I usually try to guess the client's answer and I usually run at a 50 percent accuracy rate.

This underlines the fact that you never know what you say during a session that made the biggest impact to your client.

If you can say something in a few words, please do. Power increases as the number of words decreases. If your motivation is right, and you are working to be aware of your personal dynamic, your words will likely help the client.

We Value Calibration

The art and skill of calibration is so important to us, and it's one of our core values. Here is a portion of Lead Self Lead Others' values on this topic.

- We calibrate our coaching to fit the uniqueness of our clients
    - We study our clients Birkman® and adapt accordingly.
    - We treat our clients the way they prefer to be treated.

---

[14] Proverbs 17:27 (NLT)

- o We seek ongoing feedback from our clients about our coaching.
- We engage in ongoing training, development, and evaluation of our coaching & consulting skills
- We offer our own lives as examples of people who lead themselves well

Calibration underscores the fact that coaching is an other-oriented sport. It's all about the client.

How fun is that? Your job is to put other people first.

Questions for the Coach:

Evaluate your most recent coaching session by answering the following questions related to managing your personal dynamic. How well did you manage the aspects of your personality that have the tendency to be distracting to the client?

_____
_____
_____
_____
_____
_____
_____
_____
_____
_____

Did you talk too much during the coaching session?

_____
_____
_____
_____
_____
_____
_____
_____
_____
_____

Were your facial expressions too exaggerated?

_____
_____
_____
_____
_____
_____
_____

Did you feel good about what you said, how you said it, and when you said it?

_____
_____
_____
_____
_____
_____
_____
_____
_____

Did you calibrate to the uniqueness of your client in these aspects?

- Personality
- Talking
- Facial expression
- What you wear
- How you react
- What you say. (Is this helpful and memorable?)
- How you say it
- When you say it

Chapter 10
Do I Have Enough Coaching Tools?

Coaches don't need many tools . . . unless they want to help many people in many ways.

I (Dianne) had a client who experienced a death in the family, and we paused the coaching because our objectives were focused on her career. She came to see me after the funeral and wanted to talk. My role in that "session" was to listen, ask questions, and encourage. She had never lost a close family member before. At the end of the session I said, "I have a great article for you that will help you learn about the subject of grief." When our coaching resumed, she told me how much the article helped her, and that she even shared it with other family members.

The point of this story is that I didn't write the article. But I did have it in my toolbox. And I did send it. Truth be told (and I'm a truth-teller after all) the article was certainly more helpful to her than anything I said in our meeting. And that's the goal—to help the client move forward, no matter who or what gets the credit.

Make sure your client understands the purpose of the resources and next steps. Remind them in the follow-up email. And make sure you address the exercises in your next session. We sometimes ask the client to bring up the email in the session, which reinforces accountability. After three or four sessions, when the client walks in the door, they already have their next steps up on their phone, like presenting their boarding pass at the airport.

The goal is to understand your clients and have the skills—and the tools—to help them move forward.

Build Your Toolbox

If you visited my (Nathan) office in the early days, I could have shown you my files—large drawers filled with folders filled with clippings and charts and graphs and articles and copies of resources I found helpful. Computers were expensive and few materials were digitized, so my toolbox was old-school analog. (My brain *still* is, but that's another story.)

Once the files began to overflow, it was difficult to find what I needed. So I spent a weekend pulling every resource out, organizing each by topic, and creating a filing system for easy retrieval. If a page from a book fit more than one category, I'd photocopy it and place it in each of those files.

By the way, I use these categories:

- Self-Leadership
- Habits
- Health
- Communication
- Relationships
- Time
- Money
- Leadership
- Management
- Culture
- Teamwork
- Coaching
- Spiritual Formation
- Identity
- Transition
- Manhood
- Living Well
- Finishing well

Coaching takes a lot of time but retrieving tools should not. *I have this great article but can I put my hands on it?* If a client struggled with listening skills, we'd search our "Communication" file and provide a tool that fit his need.

When we moved into the digital world, our computers were—and is—organized around coaching topics. If a client would appreciate a diagram, podcast, movie clip, or article on a certain topic, we can deliver.

We even "clip" cartoons on certain subjects, because some comic relief is often the best tool for follow-up after an intense session, or when a client pops into your mind between sessions.

What Is a Coaching Toolbox?

On a basic level, a tool box is big enough to hold a variety of tools, but small enough to be portable and usable. Have you ever started a small home-repair project that you thought only required a screwdriver, but ended up requiring eleven trips to the garage for additional tools? Almost every time, right?

Now imagine how you'd feel if the professional you hired for the job handled the project that way—or didn't have the right tools—especially if they were paid by the hour?

If a client brings up a certain situation he's struggling with, I always think about resources that might be in my toolbox to help. I'll make a note to check and include it in the follow-up.

And we often *create* tools for them.

Back to the Drawing Board

Several times a week, I (Nathan) pull out a pen and a piece of paper and draw something for the client—usually a diagram I remember seeing somewhere or one I invented. (My classic "Finishing Well" diagram has been shared tens of thousands of times by Dianne and me—and by our team of coaches.)

In every office I've ever had there's been a whiteboard or a marker pad—usually attached to the back of the office door. Most of the time clients will take a picture or ask to take the sheet of drawings with them for further review.

Diagrams are golden. They are a way to visualize a sticking point, a relationship, or the path to the objective in a simple, memorable way. In the beginning, I drew as a way to help me figure out what the client was really saying. My drawing was a way of re-stating.

103

I'm not an artist (my drawings consist of lines, squares, triangles, circles, and maybe an arrow) but I cannot tell you how many times someone has looked at my "artwork" and said, "That's exactly what the problem is. And that's what I need to focus on!"

Does every coach need to draw diagrams? No. But if you enroll in Real Coaching Success, or attend one of our workshops, you'll have an opportunity to practice.

Last month I saw a LinkedIn post from a coach we trained and certified, which included a photo of her presenting to bank executives in their boardroom. I zoomed in on the image and saw that she'd drawn one of our classic diagrams.

She literally took that tool to the bank!

Create Your Toolbox

If you're a coach, or want to be, you probably have a few books on your shelf. Take inventory and organize them according to their subject. Then do the same, on your computer, with articles, drawings, cartoons, web sites, and include anything that you find might be helpful for a current or future client.

If a resource has been helpful to you, there's an excellent chance it will be helpful to some of your clients.

If you have ten books, you now have ten tools. Add 90 articles and your toolbox now contains 100 tools. Once you start organizing, you'll find dozens of helpful materials come across your screens every week. Curate and organize them.

Just make sure your system is easy for you to retrieve when needed. We use Evernote, and it allows us to send resources directly from the application. There are many other apps on the market, but the key is for your resources to be searchable, reviewable, and retrievable. The goal is to deliver huge value for your client, and for you to invest less than 60 seconds to find and send the best tool.

The more organized you are, and the more tools you have, the better the position you are in to really help your client by delivering extra mile value.

Show us your coaching tools and we can predict your success.

Questions for the Coach:

What can you do to improve your coaching toolbox?

What subjects do you need to do some work on to build your coaching toolbox?

Chapter 11
Your Coaching Success

Coaching is work. But it's definitely not a job.

A few years ago, our dear friend, Drew asked, "Can you tell me again what you do for a living? You don't *sell* anything—so what exactly do you do?"

The biggest misconception about coaching is that most people have no idea what it is—or what it can be. Some may see this widespread lack of understanding as a challenge to their coaching business. But we see it as an opportunity.

Here's a typical conversation on an airplane.

"What line of work are you in?" someone may ask.

"I'm a leadership coach."

At this point, one of two reactions occur. First, if they have a negative stereotype of coaching, they nod their head, say "Oh. That's great," and reach for the in-flight magazine. But those are the exceptions—and not your potential clients.

Most people will ask, "What's that? You mean like a life coach?"

When they ask, it's an opportunity to define the service we provide to others.

What a responsibility—and what a privilege.

Life Change

Coaching is not about the label. It's about the results. Life change. And that's what builds a business.

Over my thirty-year career, I (Dianne) have had the honor of helping hundreds of women improve their lives and move their stories forward—step by step. I've played a small part in businesses built, careers transitioned, finances increased, and even relationships healed.

We've seen women who were petrified of "selling" go on to break sales records and train other salespeople.

Some of the women I've coached looked like they had it all together, yet struggled with confidence. Others had lots of confidence, but needed some professional business coaching in order to break through in their careers.

I became friends with many of the women I've worked with, and am often invited to lunch by them. It's amazing and humbling to me. We feel the same sense of awe when it comes to coaches we've trained. When we equip a coach for real success, there's no telling how many lives will be changed for the better.

Tag Team

A few years ago, I (Nathan) bumped into a friend from high school. We invited Julie over for dinner and caught up on life and career. She'd recently been through some difficult times in her personal life, and was looking to make a career change.

"So, what do you guys do?" came the familiar question.

We told her about coaching, but she couldn't figure it out. (Hopefully we've improved at explaining coaching since then!)

"How does this work?" she asked.

"We spend time with our clients and help them think about their purpose and potential. And then we challenge them to take their next steps. One thing we've learned, is when people go through transitions, it's a very good time for coaching because they're working through some big questions, like: *Who am I? What's next for me? What's my purpose?*"

"I need coaching. Now," she said.

Because we wanted to focus on our friendship (we don't coach friends) we referred Julie to Lori, one of the coaches we were training.

After a couple months, Lori told us that our friend, Julie was doing amazing. That didn't surprise us. What we weren't expecting was Lori telling us she thought Julie would make an awesome coach.

Julie enrolled in Real Coaching Success training, and was soon ready for a "practice client."

Kristi, a young woman Dianne and I knew, needed some coaching, and we connected her with Julie.

Fast forward a few months, and guess what? Julie told us, "I think Kristi would make a great coach!"

Yes, Kristi is now a professional coach on the Lead Self Lead Others coaching team. In two years, we saw three generations of coaches go from "What's coaching?" to invoicing clients and celebrating life change.

By the way, we have a fun tradition in our company. We ask our coaches to send a picture of their first check, and their new, highest checks to the rest of the team to encourage everyone. As we were writing this book, a text with a photo of a check came in from one of these coaches, celebrating another success. Emoji high-fives all around!

Referral Coaching Success

If you want real coaching success, combine the right motivation, professionalism, tools, and skills along with integrity and excellence. Can you imagine any business *not* succeeding with this combination?

Yes, part of success—for most coaches—is financial compensation. But it's a by-product, not the motivation.

A doctor I (Nathan) coached was so grateful for the change she experienced (mostly the result of hard work and good choices on her part) that she put together a wine social at her home, just to introduce friends and colleagues to Dianne and me.

Have you ever heard of a referral on that level? Us either, but we'll take it!

And did I mention she offered to pay me to attend? (Of course, I expressed my appreciation but declined compensation.)

Again, the currency of coaching is referrals. But on a deeper level, life change is what really *drives* the referrals.

If you want this kind of business-building energy. Please pay attention to what we're saying in this book. Study it, practice it. Build your skills and deliver excellence.

We are dealing with people's lives. For some reason people have chosen to take the courageous step of entrusting part of their life to you as their coach. What will you bring to the table?

The title of this book is *Real Coaching Success*. And if you haven't noticed by now, this phrase has two meanings. Yes, a growing business bank account with larger and larger deposits are one measure. But the *real* success is the ability to recount stories of personal transformation.

We are in the life change business.

Coaching Fuel

Julie knew zero about coaching. Today she is one of our top-earning coaches. During trainings, Julie took ferocious notes. If we blinked, she probably wrote it down in her notebook. We actually told her, "You're taking too many notes!" And she would proceed to write that down as well. Okay, we're kidding. A little. But she just couldn't get enough information because she wanted to coach with excellence.

When it was time for her to set her rates, she identified eighteen people who had expressed interest in coaching—the highest number of prospective clients we'd ever seen by a new coach.

A few weeks later we asked about the list. "Everyone said yes. All eighteen people!"

"How many are paying you?" we asked.

"Two."

"That's a lot of practice clients! We're so glad you are coaching people, but you have more value than you realize. And as soon as you can, you need to start charging all your clients."

Gradually she had more and more clients aboard the pay-train. After a few months, about half her clients were paying, and all eighteen were still engaged. Finally she called us and blurted, "Okay I'm done! This is hard work and I'm not going to coach for free anymore."

Julie finally raised her prices to our market standard. Some "free clients" didn't want to pay, which is completely normal and to be expected. But what was remarkable to see was how her energy and results skyrocketed, because she now had more margin. She could finally lead herself well, and bring more skills to her clients. Results naturally followed—along with referrals.

Best of all, she's enjoying being a coach.

Will You?

Here's our question to you: *Are you going to step into your full potential?*

You know that every person has potential, and that's why you are interested in coaching. But are you willing to go after *your own* potential? And what are you going to *do* to get there?

Part of our book development took place at a beautiful resort in the desert. After a big day of brainstorming and planning, we sat on the porch, gazed at the sunset on the red mountains, and said to each other, "Can you believe we're here, doing what we do, all because we decided to become more intentional about helping people?"

Every year we kept adding a few more tools, a few more stories, and a few more successes. We just kept going, and kept growing. Then we helped our coaches do the same.

Do you want to see what your potential is—where life might take you—if you really go after this thing called coaching?

Remember the chapter about your power messages? They often come from pain and hardship on your story. Part of my (Nathan) story is that I graduated high school with a 1.8 GPA. I was not a great student and had the grades to prove it. In most of my primary education, I never did homework and never read a book. Yes, I had so much potential, but I didn't know it.

When I somehow graduated high school, my plan was to work at an oil change shop. Why? Employees could get free services! My red, 1976 Pontiac Grand Prix—with chrome wheels and both a cassette player *and* an under-dash eight track player—had the cleanest oil in the state. I thought I hit the big time.

Thankfully, some wonderful coaches and mentors believed in my potential and drew it out of me. Nineteen years later, I graduated seminary with a doctorate and a 4.0 GPA.

When someone tells me their difficult story, I empathize with them, but I don't feel sorry for them. And I don't let them off the hook when it comes time to face their adversities. I can go toe to toe with most people when it comes to difficult circumstances. If I can make it, they can make it.

I want to help you reach your full potential, is what comes to mind when they share their life experiences. I see my story in their story.

That's why we are so bold about the concepts in this book, and the training resources we offer. They will produce results.

Your Real Success

You don't have to be perfect to be successful. But you must pursue excellence.

And success is not necessarily about income.

One of our coaches helps clients for free. She tried fee-based coaching and was paid very well, but at the end of the day she said it wasn't her calling. She wanted to provide a service for women and didn't want to charge them. However, she very much wanted to provide excellence. She embodies real coaching success.

Remember our friend Dave, who you met in chapter one. That guy never charged anyone a dime. He's still coaching me. And we no longer fight over the check at breakfast because now it's always on me.

Dave has coached thousands of people, has circled the globe teaching, training, and mentoring. He is paid well to *not* charge people for coaching. He always has at least five new stories every time we meet. And every time he tells these stories his eyes fill with tears.

Before we say goodbye, he says—with his trademark smile—"Can you believe we get to do this? Isn't this awesome? Isn't this fun?!"

Coaching is *work*. Hard work. But it's definitely not a *job*.

The Next Step

If you have a natural drive toward being intentional about helping other grow, you are a coach—even if you don't use the term.

Can you turn that drive into a thriving business? Of course you can. The real question is, *will you?*

People are waiting for someone exactly like you to help move their story forward.

What are you waiting for?

Come join us!

Questions for the Coach:

How do you describe what you do as a coach to those who ask?

___

Over the last year, how many of your clients have come directly from a referral?

___

What do you believe is your potential is as a coach?

_____
_____
_____
_____
_____
_____
_____
_____

After reading this book, and answering the questions in each chapter, in what areas do you need the most help to experience real coaching success?

_____
_____
_____
_____
_____
_____
_____
_____

Dr. Nathan Baxter

Nathan has been coaching leaders for over 30 years. In the fall of 2001 he and his wife, Dianne founded Lead Self Lead Others.

To date they have successfully coached over 3,500 leaders, issued over two thousand Birkman® assessments and 360 performance evaluations, and designed and conducted hundreds of individual and corporate surveys.

Dr. Baxter and Dianne realized that there were many others who were interested in learning about their coaching model and methodology. Real Coaching Success was founded in 2014 to help other coaches realize their full potential, and serve others with excellence.

They have worked in a variety of industries including Banking, Real Estate, Cryogenics, Medical, Oil & Gas, Public Accounting, Engineering, Industrial Supply, Sales, Athletic Equipment, Direct Sales, Universities, Schools, and Churches, to name a few. They've provided services for clients and coaches in twenty states and three countries.

Nathan has been married to Dianne for 33 years and have two sons, two daughters-in-law, and three grandchildren.

Dianne Baxter

Dianne has been coaching women in her successful business for over 30 years, and helped hundreds of women start and grow their own businesses. She earned a Bachelor of Science degree in Marketing from Oklahoma State University.

In 2014, she and her husband, Nathan decided to start helping others who were interested in coaching by hosting a two-day workshop in their home, as a way to teach their coaching tips, tools, and techniques and inspire other coaches to develop their own unique coaching practice. This has since grown into an annual Coaching Success Workshop, online learning, and coaching certification for Real Coaching Success.

She and Nathan have been married for 33 years and have two sons, two daughters-in-law, and three grandchildren.

Glossary of our coaching terminology:

We developed these terms and definitions to help us communicate with one another and to our coaching team.

Accountability: The act of helping another person accomplish what they are capable of doing.

Active Listening: When a coach uses all of their skills to fully understand their client's point of view. This can include asking clarifying questions, making mental notes of phrases or comments, and observing their body language.

Birkman® Assessment: The Birkman Method® describes desires, strengths, motivational needs and stress reactions for the individual and provides basic recommendations for developing skills when faced with varying environments and people. Contact www.RealCoachingsuccess.com to learn more about using this tool to deliver excellence.

Calibration: The adjustment a coach makes to best relate to their client's interests, usual behavior, and hidden needs.

Client Experience Survey: A survey completed by a coaching client indicating their experience of the coaching engagement. Contact us to lean more about this tool.

Client Hack: A client hack is a tip, trick, or process that a coach has learned to better engage their client.

Coaching: The intentional act of one person coming alongside another person to help them continuously move toward their full potential.

Coaching Engagement: A defined relationship between a coach and their client that is documented in a coaching proposal.

Coaching Excellence: Coaching excellence occurs when a coach consistently engages the client in a way that moves client along the coaching engagement to achieve the coaching objectives.

Coaching Objectives: Specific change goals identified at the beginning of a coaching engagement.

Coaching Gap: The distance between a person's potential and their current reality that they have worked with their coach to identify.

Coaching Proposal: A written document a coach creates for a potential client that includes coaching objectives, process for coaching, estimated coaching duration and costs for services.

Coaching Session: A description of the total time spent working with a client that includes pre-session work and preparation, in-session work and conversation, and post-session work and follow up.

Coaching Relationship Dynamic: The unique way a coach and client relate to one another.

Coaching Toolbox: A collection of resources that a coach has at their disposal and can use as needed to achieve the coaching objectives.

Coaching uniqueness: The unique coaching style and approach that each coach develops and uses when working with their clients.

Counseling: The act of one person coming alongside another person to help them repair damage from their past and discover how to cope with their current life.

Critical Focus List (CFL): A simple list that a coach helps their client create and maintain, that contains "who" and "what" they must focus on in order to move their story forward.

Custom Coaching: Custom coaching occurs when the coach creates a unique coaching plan to fit the unique needs of their client that rarely can be used on another client. Lead Self Lead Others only engages in custom coaching.

Duration: The estimated time the coaching engagement will last, which is identified before the coaching begins.

Emotional Intelligence: Emotional intelligence is your ability to recognize and understand emotions in yourself and others, and your ability to use this awareness to manage your behavior and relationships. (*Emotional Intelligence 2.0*, page 17)

Finishing Well: A short phrase that represents the desired finish a client wants to achieve and experience. This phrase can be used to help a client think about how they want to finish their week, month, year, career—and their life.

Finishing Well Diagram: Dr. Baxter's coaching model that he, Dianne, and their team of coaches use at Lead Self Lead Others to guide their clients to experience their full potential. The core components include potential, current reality, pushbacks, story, uniqueness, hard wiring, coaching plan with next steps, living well, finishing well, and eternity. Contact us to learn more.

Follow-Up Note: A summary of the coaching conversation created by the coach and sent to their client within 24–48 hours of the session. The note should contain encouraging words, truth, progress observed, and a list of their next steps.

Fog Cutting Questions: A question or questions that are co-created by the coach and their client, and used during each coaching session to help cut through the fog of excuses for not completing their next steps.

Frustration Gap: The emotion of frustration experienced when a person becomes aware of the gap between their current reality and their preferred future that is based on their potential.

Golden Rule: Treat other people that way you want to be treated. See also Platinum Rule.

Lead Self Lead Others: A coaching and consulting firm that helps individuals and organizations move their stories forward. Their core premise is: if you want to lead others well then you must first lead yourself well.

Life Purpose: Summary of a client's understanding as to why they were put on the earth.

Listen to Understand: The work required for a coach to understand what their client is really saying.

Living Well: The life experience of a person who consistently works at closing the gap between their potential and their reality.

Mentoring: The act of one person sharing information, and/or life experiences, with another person for the purpose of helping them in their journey.

Next Step Exercises: The exercises a coach provides to their client to help them know what they are to do next in order to continue to move toward their full potential.

Over-coaching: Over-coaching occurs when a coach doesn't allow the client enough time to think through or experience an idea or growth exercise. In other words, the coach does the work the client should be doing.

Personal Dynamic: The experience others have when they encounter you. This dynamic can be intentional or unintentional.

Plateau: A life experience that is not satisfying because you are no longer moving toward your God-given potential.

Platinum Rule: Treat other people the way they *prefer* to be treated (Several sources claim to have invented this term. Dr. Baxter first heard it during his Birkman Certification training in 2016).

Power Message: A truth or principle that a person is passionate about because they learned it through experience.

Real Coaching Success: Real Coaching Success occurs when a coach continually receives referrals because of successful coaching engagements.

Re-engagement: When a former client decides to start a new coaching engagement with their coach.

Referral: When a coach is contacted by a potential client as a result of a positive conversation with a former client of the coach.

Self-Leadership: When a person knows what to do, when to do it, and is willing to get it done. Knowing what to do, when to do it, and being willing to get it done in order to move toward your full potential and live and finish well.

Signature Coaching Style: A description of a coach's unique style and method of coaching their clients.

Stewardship: The intentional effort of a person to manage what has been given to them. Which could include their resources, story, time, passions, uniqueness, dreams and aspirations, and their potential.

Story: A collection of experiences in a person's life that has played a role into shaping them into the person they are today.

Timeline exercise: A personal growth exercise that guides a person to review the major life-impact moments or seasons, both positive and negative, and uses the information to help them move their stories forward.

Truth-teller: A coach who identifies truths and observations about their client and skillfully shares those with them.

Appendix A

Examples of Coaching Values

We believe that every coach should develop their own set of values and refer to them often. This will help ensure consistent coaching excellence.

Here are our values at Lead Self Lead Others:

We create custom coaching and consulting plans for our clients

- We use a great intake process.
- We are willing to do the work to create a unique coaching plan for every client.
- We invite collaboration from the LSLO coaching team.

We manage time well

- We are prepared for our coaching sessions.
- We start and stop on time.
- We respond to our clients in a timely manner.

We calibrate our coaching to fit the uniqueness of our clients

- We study our client's Birkman® and adapt accordingly.
- We treat our clients the way they prefer to be treated.
- We seek ongoing feedback from our clients about our coaching.

We are truth tellers

- We value client discovery but we do not shy away from telling them the truth.
- We believe truth is what people are really seeking.

www.LeadSelfLeadOthers.com

Real Coaching Success Coaching Values

Our Values

- We want to help others develop their own unique coaching style.
- We desire to provide excellent training and resources that is affordable.
- We create resources and services that have been properly field tested and we know they work.
- We work hard to keep our resources user friendly.
- We believe that coaches need to spend time together and learn from one another.

RealCoachingSuccess.com

Appendix B

Example of Template for Taking Notes During a Coaching Session

Taking notes is one of the critical skills for successful coaching and one of the practices we work on during our RCS coaching certification training. Below is how Dr. Baxter organizes his notes on one page during a coaching session.

- Name of client
- Date of the session
- Next steps for the clients to take (their assignment)
- Notes about my client
- Next steps I need to do for my client (coaches action items)

First I place the clients name and date on the paper because you'd be surprised how easy it is to get the notes mixed up.

Second, I add any bio information I find interesting. If the client mentions they attended a certain university, or they love to boat, or something that's unique, I write that down.

Third, I write down anything related to helping them take their next step. If I'm listening to the client and don't want to interrupt their thought, I'll make a note of that.

Fourth, I note items I need to do for the client. For example, if I need to make a phone call for them, or send a resource.

That's all I write down. And I never write anything down that I would not show the client if they ask. (And some clients will ask!) When I prepare the follow-up email, the important aspects are clearly written in my notes.

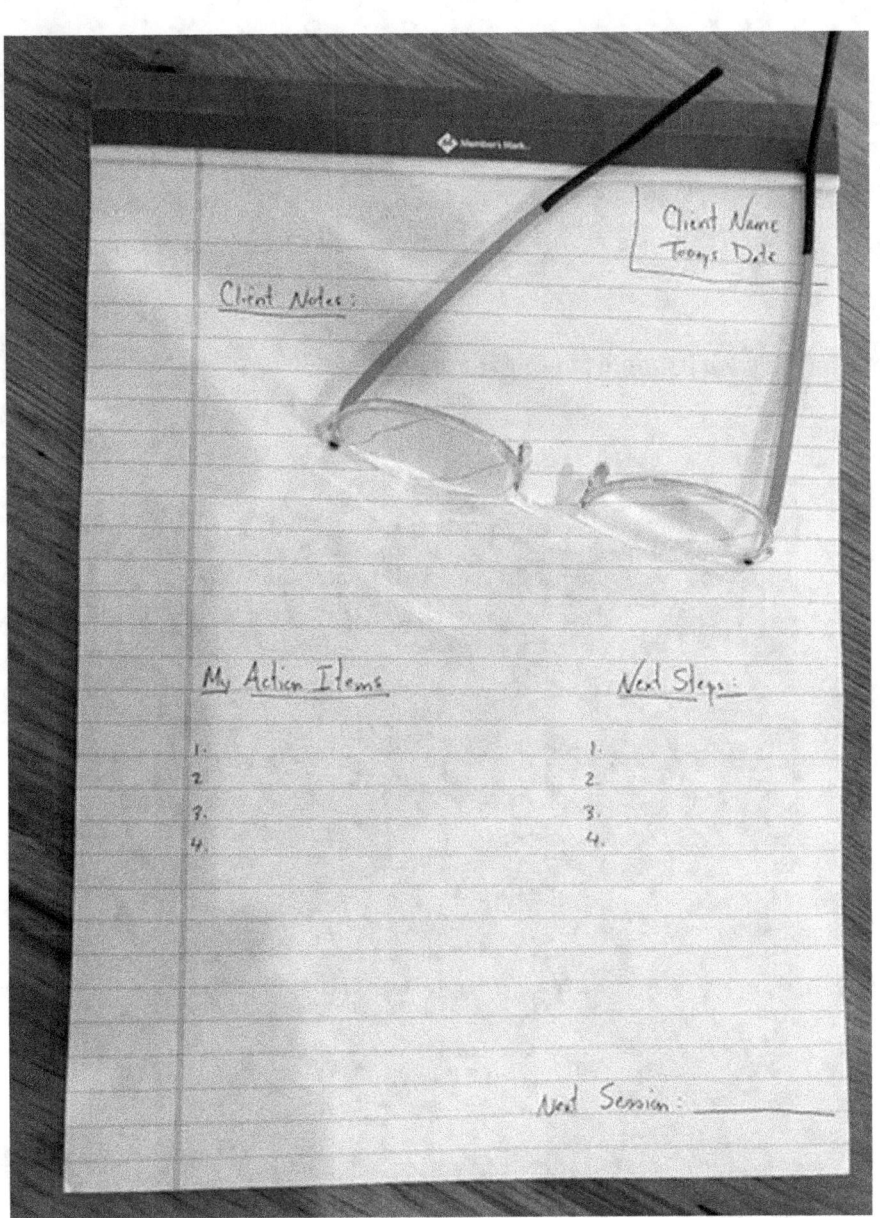

Appendix C

Using the Birkman® to identify our signature coaching style

One of biggest challenges is helping new coaches find their signature coaching style. The Birkman Method® assessment is a great tool and it is where we always begin in the RCS coaching training. Below are examples of how Dr. Baxter and Dianne developed their unique styles.

Dianne's Birkman Map® overview

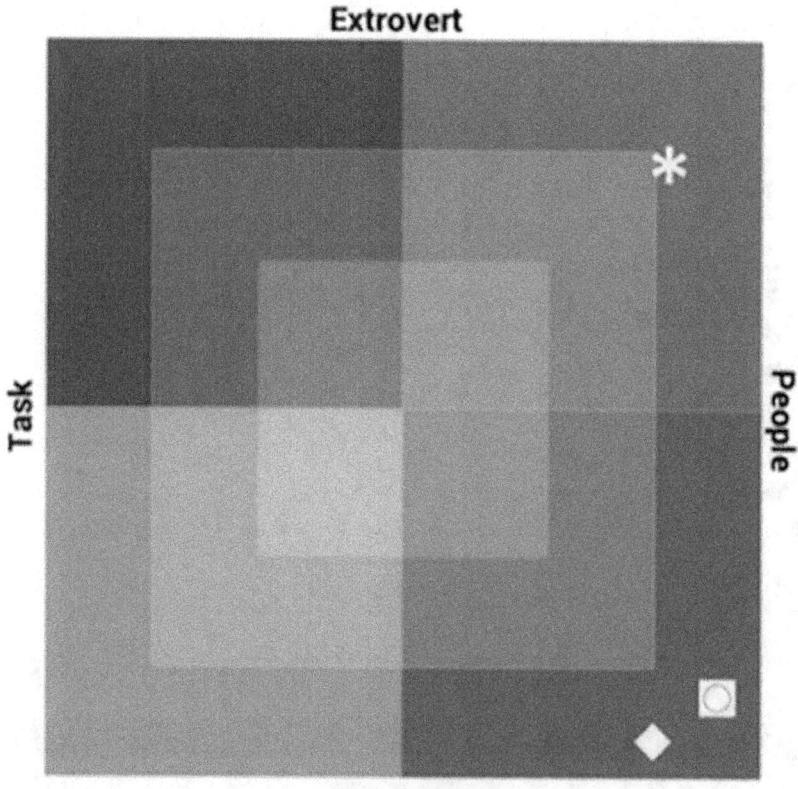

© Birkman International ® Used with permission

Dianne's natural coaching style is relational and a natural encourager. Notice all her symbols are on the right side or people side of the map. She needs to develop a strong connection with whoever she is working with. Her style works against her when she needs to focus more on the task at hand and holding others accountable because of her concern of disrupting the relationship. Also, because she has an intense need to not be over scheduled, she has to limit the amount of people she works with.

Her Interests (Asterisk)

- Extrovert / People Focused
- Easily connects with strangers. Great for generating new clients.
- Comfortable being in front of people. Naturally wired for group coaching.
- Likes to have fun and persuade people. Easily converts prospects into paying clients.

Strengths (Diamond)

- Introvert / People
- Insightful, thoughtful, and reflective. Great for listening and empathizing with clients.
- Selectively social. Able to focus on the person in front of her with ease.

Hidden Needs: (Circle)

- Introvert / People
- Needs plenty of time to make decisions. Tends to overthink what to say or not say to a client.
- Doesn't do well when over scheduled. She had to learn a good weekly coaching rhythm.

Nathan's Birkman Map® overview

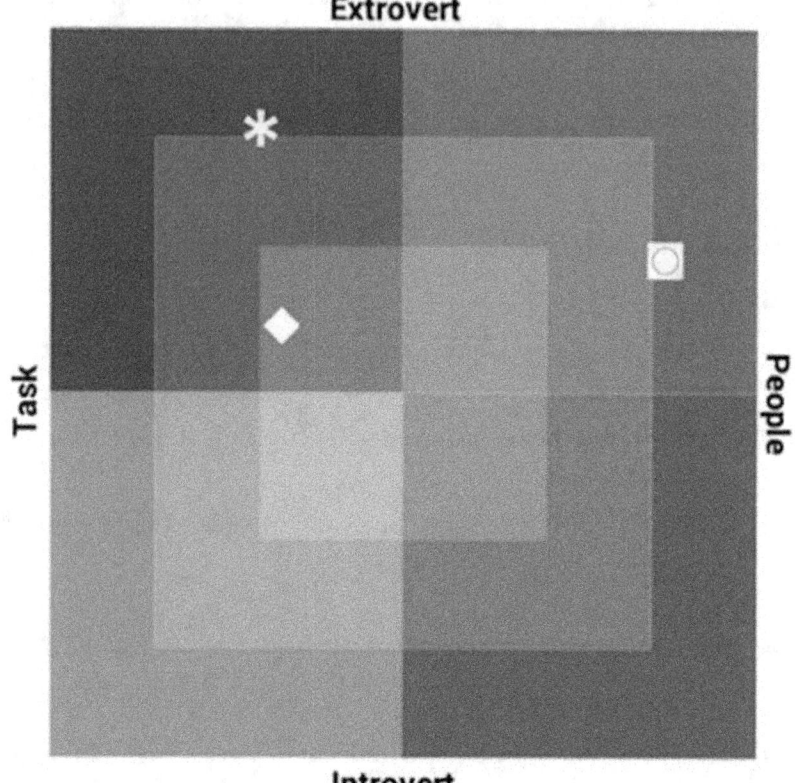

© Birkman International ® Used with permission

Nathan's natural coaching style is focused on the progress, process, and action steps. He needs to have a clear sense of coaching objectives before he can do his best work. The relationship is secondary to the task at hand. He is able to protect the relationship by consistently delivering results for his clients. His natural challenges are listening for understanding before offering direction too quickly. Also, he has had to learn to be more patient with the lack of action or progress on behalf of his clients.

His Interests (Asterisk)

- Extrovert / Task Focused
- Can easily stay focused on a process and task completion. He is motivated to help clients stay on task and great for generating new clients.
- Has a natural authoritative style. Leaders respond well to him.

Strengths (Diamond)

- Task / Centered positioned
- Relates well to clients who are wired differently than he is.
- Thinks quickly on his feet and is able to offer clients direction in the moment.

Hidden Needs: (Circle)

- Extrovert / People
- Has a high need for respect. Can be challenging to work with clients who are very self-oriented.
- Has a high need to control his schedule. Struggles to be flexible to adjust to the schedule request of his clients.

These insights represent only a tiny fraction of what the Birkman Method® assessment, and our training, provides. Contact us to learn more.

Acknowledgements

From Nathan:

      Thanks to Dave Jewitt, Paul Taylor, and Charlie Baker who took time to mentor and coach me during critical seasons of my life. To authors, Paul Stanley and Bobby Clinton, thank you for helping me find the vocabulary for my passion for coaching. Thanks to all of the Lead Self Lead Others coaches and our office team who help us faithfully serve our clients. Thanks to Mike Loomis who knew us when all we had were some unorganized ideas, and he coached us through the launching of our companies and this book. Thank you, Dianne—my wife and business partner—for partnering on this project. Excited for our next one.

From Dianne:

      Thanks to the Clark family who let us stay with them and use their boardroom for our first official conversation about getting into coaching. To Jan Thetford, thank you for leading and mentoring me with excellence. Thanks to all our assistants over the years who allowed us to stay focused on what we do best. We could not have made it without you. Thank you, Nathan—for countless hours watching the boys, cooking, filling up my car, etc. in the early years so that I could coach and mentor women.

lead self lead others®

moving your story forward

We have successfully coached over 3,500 leaders, issued 1800+ Birkman® assessments and 360 performance evaluations, designed and conducted over 200 surveys to help companies measure their strength of workplace and culture for their employees.

Our Vision is to be an industry leader for coaching & consulting excellence.

Our Mission is to coach and consult companies and people to move their stories forward and experience their full potential.

www.LeadSelfLeadOthers.com

Real Coaching Success

We. Equip. Coaches.

Are you ready to take the next step for Real Coaching Success?

Real Coaching Success equips coaches and mentors develop their skills and increase their success in coaching. We provide resources that equip and encourage professional *and* volunteer coaches.

Our Values:

- We want to help others develop their own unique coaching style.
- We desire to provide excellent training and resources that are affordable.
- We create resources and services that have been properly field tested and we know they work.
- We work hard to keep our resources user friendly.
- We believe that coaches need to spend time together and learn from one another.

Our mission is very simple:

To equip others to experience success in their coaching and mentoring. We do this through training, coaching, hosting gatherings of coaches at workshops, and our annual Real Coaching Success workshops. We also provide a coaching certification process and online coaching courses.

Simply contact us through our web site, and subscribe to our free newsletter.

RealCoachingSuccess.com

Join Us for Our Real Coaching Success Workshops

Coaching can be a lonely profession at times. Do you have a community for support and growth?

Dr. Baxter, Dianne, and Lead Self Lead Others coaches will guide you through the following topics, and more!

- Steps to starting a coaching business.
- Coaching for free or for a fee?
- Essentials of a great coaching tool box.
- How to build your coaching business and set your coaching fees.
- How to brand yourself and best social media practices.
- Tips for getting maximum coaching impact using the Birkman® assessment.
- Key components of a great coaching proposal.
- How to take your listening skills to the next level.
- How to earn referrals.

Subscribe for email updates about live and virtual events at:

RealCoachingSuccess.com

Contact us to learn more about:

Build Your Skills and Your Business

Real Coaching Success offers several ways to continue your journey to excellence. Contact us to learn more about:

Birkman ® Assessment and Training:

Receive your own assessment, and learn how to implement the findings to help you discover your signature coaching style—as well as how to help your clients maximize *their* reports.

Real Coaching Success Certification:

We offer a coaching certification that adapts to the need of each individual who wants to be trained in our methods and processes. We have the ability to equip someone brand new to coaching as well as coaches who have been in the business a while. Our team will help design the training process to help each person achieve their goals.

Coaching for Coaches:

Personal consultation with you to answer questions, get unstuck, and reach your potential.

RealCoachingSuccess.com

www.ingramcontent.com/pod-product-compliance
Lightning Source LLC
Chambersburg PA
CBHW060841220526
45466CB00003B/1198